TONY MCNALL

STILL WATC

BURN

Tony McNally

© Tony McNally 2016

Contents

<u>Dedication</u>

This book is dedicated to the men who died aboard the RFA *Sir Galahad and Sir Tristram*, and to all those killed and those injured physically or mentally in the Falklands War and more recent conflicts.

Foreword

At first sight, The Falklands is not the sort of place you'd imagine wars being fought over – a group of 700 or so bleak, hilly, windswept islands, roughly half the size of Wales, sitting in the freezing South Atlantic around 400 miles from the South American mainland.

They possess a beauty, of sorts, but you have to be a true connoisseur of wilderness to appreciate it: whichever way you look, all you see are miles and miles of empty, undulating, grey-green grasslands, granite and scars of dark, peaty soil in which no indigenous trees grow.

It never gets very hot – even in January, at the height of the southern hemisphere summer, it's barely above 70 degrees Fahrenheit – and, while the sun shines weakly down for much of the year, it's often bitterly cold, especially when the biting wind blows up from the Antarctic circle a few hundred miles south.

There's fishing, and sheep farming, and – possibly – offshore oil at some point in the future, but there are no hidden riches, no goldmines, not ever any particular strategic significance to the place.

But it is British, whatever Argentina may think, and the people who live there look to us for their protection.

The Argentineans have long claimed the islands as their own, but they were discovered by an Englishman, Captain John Davis in the ship *Desire*, in August 1592. The first recorded landing was made in 1690 by another English sailor, Captain John Strong, who named the channel dividing the two main islands 'Falkland Sound' after Viscount Falkland, the Royal Navy's treasurer. The British took formal possession of the islands for the Crown in 1765 – fully 51 years before Argentina even existed – and, although there was some to-ing and fro-ing with the French and Spanish governments over the next few decades, they were never relinquished.

A permanent British presence was established on the islands in 1833 and our administration remained unbroken from then until now.

Apart from ten weeks in 1982.

This is the story of my small part in ending the Argentinean occupation of the Falklands 34 years ago – about how I found myself in the Army and on those islands so far from home, what I did there and how that changed my life forever.

The official figures show that over 250 British soldiers and Falkland Islanders died in the war, together with more than 1,000 Argentineans.

Many people have wondered whether that empty toehold in the southern ocean was worth all those deaths.

Tragic as they were, I'm not one of them.

I think the Falklands were worth fighting for, I'm proud I got the chance to take part and I'd do it all again in an instant.

DEATH FROM ABOVE

THE noise was unbelievably quick and almost paralysingly loud, and the terror it brought – fleeting though it was – was mind-numbing. Until you've been attacked by a fast jet bomber, you can't imagine what it's like. Forget the movies, they're a joke – even standing at the end of an airport runway and listening to the big 747s come and go doesn't come anywhere near.

The plane passed over us at a height of around 30 feet – he'd have knocked the chimney pots off my house back home – and doing well over 600 miles an hour.

At low level and at that speed, the sound of its howling turbofan engine was here and gone in a matter of seconds, like a deafening, horrifying thunderclap that turned my insides to mush.

The almost overwhelming urge, if you have time, is to hide – to dive into a trench, to get behind rocks, to find some sort of cover – but that's not an option for professional soldiers.

And it certainly wasn't an option for Rapier missile operators. Our job was to do the exact opposite: to sit there, naked to the world, in the hot seat of the system, and try to shoot the enemy down. It wasn't a comfortable experience. Our positions were always highly exposed and our camouflage was next to non-existent, and the pilots knew what we had in mind.

This one had come over the hill behind us just after we finished our T's and A's, (Tests and adjustments), sticking to the contours of the land to make it even harder for us to hit him, and banking away in search of our ships as he passed above.

I could see the word 'Armada' stencilled on the side of the white-bellied plane, and the bombs on his underside, and the helmeted head of the pilot turned downwards to look at us.

Then he was gone, leaving nothing but his down-draft, the hot smell of kerosene exhaust and a loud ringing in my ears.

Nearby, a platoon of infantrymen were yelling abuse and letting rip with their SLRs and a GPMG – several hundred rounds disappearing into the pale blue sky in a futile gesture of defiance. It's extremely hard to hit a fast jet with a rifle, but the boys were having a good go.

To my right, one of our missiles roared off the beam as Quinny engaged the Argentinean, but he pulled right and disappeared around the headland and away to safety and the missile fell harmlessly into the sea.

I watched him all the way as he streaked out of sight, and silently thanked God that he had other targets in mind that day.

The unlucky ones didn't get that chance: at those speeds, if he's on his bombing run and he knows what he's doing, by the time you've heard the jet you're already on your way to the next world, propelled there by a couple of tonnes of high explosive and a vicious hail of supersonic steel shrapnel. That was my introduction to the A4 Skyhawk – one of a number of planes thrown at us by the Argentineans during the Falklands War. The A4 was a 40 foot, eight tonne workhorse of a killer which would go on to wreak havoc on our shipping during the conflict, destroying the *Coventry*, the *Antelope* and the *Sir Galahad*, and taking a lot of good lads with them. A number of pilots lost their own lives, flying with an almost reckless bravery that you had to admire – even while you hated the bastards and wanted them all dead.

As the sound of the disappearing jet blended into the background noise of the wind and the calling seagulls, I got on with digging my trench – we'd only landed on the Falklands a couple of hours before.

And as I dug, my mind was buzzing with adrenalin, and my heart was still thumping in my chest. Although we'd had an air raid warning, I hadn't heard a thing until he was almost on top of us and the reaction time was close to zero. If we'd ever entertained any doubts that this war was the real thing, and that people were going to die, they were surely gone now.

This was deadly serious.

SERVING THE APPRENTICESHIP

I grew up in Cumbria, an area of rugged landscapes and white-flecked seas not unlike the Falklands in appearance. I was born on the 11th July 1962, at Risedale maternity hospital in Barrow- in- Furness, and was brought up on a council estate in the nearby small market town of Dalton.

My parents were both Irish Catholics from Dublin – my mother was a deeply religious woman, with a rosary never far from her hand, and my father a hard worker who liked a pint of Guinness or three in the evenings. There was never much money around, and times were tough, though they would get tougher for everyone as the shipbuilding and iron industries began their decline after the high water mark of the middle of the century.

Dalton sits high on a peninsula which juts out into Morecambe Bay and on calm, clear days you feel like you can see forever. To the south, across the bay, you can see Morecambe and Lancaster, to the north, the sweeping hills and valleys of the Lake District, wild and beautiful countryside where I spent a lot of my childhood. To the west, out into the Irish Sea, we'd watch huge ships built in

Barrow setting off on their maiden voyages: among them may well have been the *HMS Sheffield*, laid down in the Vickers yard in 1970. She'd be famous a dozen years later, for all the wrong reasons.

I went to Dowdales Comprehensive School and achieved four CSEs; I wasn't the most academic of lads, and the best of my results was a Grade One in English, but that didn't worry me too much. Since I'd been a young boy, I'd wanted to be a soldier. Like a lot of boys I had a fascination for toy guns, tanks, planes, anything military, and would while away the hours staging my own wars in the back yard, destroying whole divisions of plastic German or Japanese infantry in one fell swoop with a spud gun or a big mud ball. I can remember my Mam scolding me many times for the state of my clothes and for the mess I'd made of the garden. What did I care? I'd just won the battle of Arnhem. (Little did I realise, at the time, what great practice this would be for a career in the British Army – the getting-bollocked-and-sweeping-mud-off-paths bit, that is).

My first organised military involvement was with the Army cadets of the Kings Own Royal Border Regiment, which I joined at around 14. The change in me was remarkable: overnight, I went from being a spotty, skinny, long-haired teenager to being a spotty, skinny, short-haired teenager.

My mate George and I were soon staging clandestine Commando raids on local targets. We would sneak quietly out of our houses at 0200hrs in the dead of night, dressed in our cadet combats, cam-cream smudged on our faces to keep us hidden in the darkness, in search of adventure. Back then, in 1976, we were at the height of the Cold War, and the threat from Russia and the Soviet Union felt very real; we'd spend the wee small hours outwitting the evil Communist enemy (or Cumbria Constabulary, as some knew them) and wreaking havoc on the better-kept gardens in Dalton's snootier parts. Our favourite mission involved finding small trees, digging them up and then re-planting them a few doors down. We'd wet ourselves laughing thinking of folks' faces when they opened the front door in the morning and found a small apple tree had miraculously sprung up overnight. One high-level enemy target was our music teacher, code-named 'Mr Porter'. We bust our guts for weeks laughing about how he must have struggled to prise his super-glued milk bottles from his doorstep.

We thought we were bad lads, and if you'd have asked Mr Porter he'd have probably agreed, but, in hindsight, these pranks were pretty minor stuff by today's standards.

My fascination with uniforms, rifles, loud bangs, and crawling around in shit led to the inevitable: at the tender age of 16, and much to my mother's disappointment, I joined the British Army, enlisting on August 14, 1978.

The Army posted me a rail warrant and I said goodbye to my tearful Mam, walking down the hill to the station and feeling all excited and grown-up. I took the two-hour train journey up the coast to Carlisle, stopping at stations I had never even heard of, before we got to where we were going and I took a taxi to the Army Careers Office in town. I was given a card to read the oath of allegiance:

'I swear, by Almighty God, that I will be faithful and bear true allegiance to Her Majesty Queen Elizabeth the Second, her Heirs and successors, and that I will as in duty bound, honestly and faithfully defend Her Majesty, her

*Heirs and successors, in person, Crown and dignity
against all enemies, and will observe and obey all orders
of Her Majesty, Her Heirs and successors, and of the
officers set over me, so help me God.'*

In earlier times, recruits to the Army had signed on
the dotted line and been given a shilling in return – hence
the expression, 'taking the Queen's Shilling'. Well, the
Queen can't have been feeling too flush that day because I
didn't get a shilling. I didn't even get tuppence, but the
ACIO (Army Careers Information Officer), a big sergeant
smelling of spray starch and boot polish, did give me a cup
of weak coffee and a friendly nod.

I became Junior Leader McNally of the Royal
Regiment of Artillery, based at the Gamecock Barracks at
Bramcote, near Nuneaton in Warwickshire. Why the Royal
Artillery? Well, the man in the careers office was a Gunner;
if he'd been in the Catering Corps, this book would
possibly be about my unique recipe for pea and ham soup
and how its introduction into the Army diet fundamentally
changed the culinary perspective of the average squaddie.

The Junior Leader Regiments, or Brats as they are
affectionately known, were set up to create potential future

leaders of men, the British Army's famous NCOs (Non-Commissioned Officers). In simpler terms, these are the ugly bastards with the stripes on their arms and the big sticks, screaming in your ears and kicking you up the arse on cross country runs.

Basic training wasn't all that glamorous, particularly early on. It was basic and it was training, and that's about it.

I had a bit of a head start over some of the lads because, having been in the Army cadets, I already knew how to march and bull my boots. (Incidentally, you'll hear a lot of old soldiers talking of 'spit and polish' being the best way to shine boots. In my opinion, that's a load of rubbish. Spit is greasy and it takes you forever to get a good finish. Take it from me, the best way is just to put a little fresh water into the lid of your polish tin, dip your bulling rag in the polish, then in the water and away you go. How it works I have no idea but it definitely does and though it does take a lot of practice it's a bit like riding a bike: once you have mastered it, you never forget.)

Alongside the marching and boot-cleaning, there was also plenty of cleaning the block, personal admin, ironing, cleaning the block, more marching and more cleaning the block. If you've ever spent time in the Army you will never forget the smell of the yellow wax polish liberally applied to linoleum floors; by the time we'd finished they were so clean your Granny could eat her dinner off them. In between the cleaning, we also learned how to fire a rifle. Although my destination was 12 Air Defence Regt RA, a unit that used Rapier missiles in an air defence role, we had to be able to join in an infantry attack if necessary, or defend our unit and ourselves if we were attacked. In those days, the Army's basic weapon was the L1A1 SLR (Self-Loading Rifle), the British version of the Belgian FN FAL. To a young lad weaned on war comics, this was an exciting bit of kit: the SLR was an excellent and very popular weapon, a highly-accurate, gas-operated, semi-automatic, magazine-fed killer. If you wanted to fire a round, you simply squeezed the trigger and one would arrive from the magazine and depart through the muzzle. This was a major advance from the old, wooden Lee Enfield .303 that I had learned to fire in the cadets, which required you to work a bolt to chamber the bullet. The SLR fired a 7.62mm round, and gave you a good kick in your shoulder with the recoil; we quickly learned to keep the butt tight to our bodies, because the impact of the butt can break a man's shoulder or collar bone if he's unprepared. It does a lot more damage than that at the other end, of course: I remember watching the instructor fondling his rifle and almost drooling about its killing power at ranges of 600 metres and more.

If you were unfortunate to fail any aspect of your basic training you could find yourself 'back-squadded', and having to go through the whole thing again with the new recruits. Luckily, I managed to avoid this fate and progressed to my trade training, Gunnery.

For me, this was the best part of my twelve months' training, especially the bits where we learned how to fire large pieces of metal, with lots of different nasty surprises inside, over long distances so that they would land on the heads of lads who were just like me, but only from Russia.

We didn't know it then, but we were to be the last intake to learn our trade on 25 pounders, one of the best artillery pieces used by the British Army and a mainstay of our troops in the Second World War. This gun weighed 1.8 tonnes but that felt like twenty tonnes when you had to run around the football field pushing the bastard after fucking up laying (aiming) the gun properly. Worst of all was if you were laying the gun in an anti-tank role in the gunnery hangar. There was a small wooden tank on the other side of the hangar and the idea was that you looked at it through the sight and lined it up, slap bang in the middle. Once you finished, you moved away so that your Number One (NCO) would apply his critical eye to the sight. This was a very nervous time and the nerves only increased as he pulled away and invited you to take another look. You would put your eye back to the sight, a large fist would then smash your head into it and stars would erupt all around you. Then you would set off around the football pitch, dragging your 25 pounder, nursing a black eye and wondering how far you'd been from the centre of that fucking wooden tank.

We lived in fear of the NCOs; the Army can be a pretty harsh environment, though I never really suffered too much. If you had the audacity to lose step while marching, or be found with a contraband orange hidden under your armpit after meal times, you'd be put on punishment parade to get you back on the straight and narrow. Punishment parade consisted of standing to attention on one leg for as long as humanly possible under the watchful gaze of our Drill Sergeant Major, a Scots Guardsman. I know that doesn't sound too bad on paper but God didn't design us with two legs for no reason and, eventually, somebody's other foot would touch the floor. The Drill Sergeant Major, the most frightening man I had ever encountered in all my 16 years on this planet, was a guy so psychopathically scary even our training NCOs seemed almost apologetic when they told us we had him for drill. On seeing this foot touch down, he would break into convulsions, like a psychopath with a bad case of St Vitus Dance, and make you do the whole thing again for another hour. Weaker soldiers who collapsed were kicked and punched and struck over the head with a pace stick.

This punishment parade was held on a weekly basis, until the Commanding Officer's wife, while out walking her dogs, noticed us being tortured in this manner and promptly let her hubby know her feelings on the matter. The end result was that the phrase 'punishment parade' was quietly changed to 'extra drill parade', the practice of using two feet on the ground was adopted and the punching and kicking was gradually phased out.

My Mam, God bless her, used to send me a food parcel now and again, containing lots of goodies and the local paper. Once a week, we'd all line up for our mail outside the troop office and wait for our names to be called out.

'McNally,' Sergeant Laycock would say, his voice dripping with sarcasm. 'Your mammy has been good enough to send us a food parcel. Isn't that sweet of her?'

'Yes, Sar'nt.'

'Let's have a look, shall we?'

He would then tear the parcel to pieces and I'd have to watch as he scoffed all the choccies; if I were lucky I'd get the odd sweet and *The North West Evening Mail* to read. It really pissed me off – I'd rather not have had the sodding things than have to watch Laycock cramming it all down his neck, and getting them tweaked my homesickness, too – but there was no way I was going to let the bastard see. I was determined to see this thing through. I couldn't have quit and gone back home, a failure to my mates and my family and, more importantly, to myself.

One night the rumour was we were being taken to the NAAFI shop – a bit like your average local corner shop, but with a lot more polish, starch, Brasso and other cleaning materials on sale – for a treat. We fell in outside in a state of high excitement.

'By the front, quick march.'

Off we went, mouths watering.

The rumour turned out to be quite true. We arrived at the shop and halted before being allowed to view the vast racks of sweeties and other goodies winking back at us. Then we about-turned and quick-marched back to where we had started off from, leaving 40 starving squaddies, salivating and tummies a-rumbling, the cruel bastards.

It's weird how desperate you get for sweets and fizzy pop. The senior Gunners – who were allowed perks, like access to the NAAFI and nights out on the lash – would flog us sips of Coke or Pepsi for 50p (about £2 in today's money). Just enough to wet the whistle and keep you keen. If you fancied a Mars bar, this would cost £1.50

and you'd better ram it down your throat double quick because if you attempted to savour it a hungry pack of rabid hyenas (i.e. your mates) would descend upon you and rip it from you in seconds. It was a nightmare, though when we became senior Gunners we naturally continued this profitable and noble tradition.

I remember a morning inspection, where a lad was picked up for having a crease in the wrong place on his shirt. He was loudly told by the Sergeant that he had ten seconds to get into the block and iron it properly. The panic-stricken soldier legged it inside, plugged in the iron and proceeded to press the shirt while it was still on his back. He ended up in the medical centre with serious burns but, to be fair, his uniform looked immaculate.

From time to time, we'd leave the questionable comforts of Bramcote and head out for adventure training. One trip, to a place called Dolweddelan in the middle of Wales' most nowhere bits, is burned into is burned into my memory. As well as the usual rock-climbing and map-reading, there was another aspect to this training that we were dreading; we had heard horror stories from other recruits about 'The Stream'. We soon found out they were all true. It was around February when we went there, so not exactly tropical. At around 0500 hours one morning, the NCOs kicked open the stable doors of our accommodation and dragged us out of bed, screaming 'Get outside'.

We had 10 seconds or something equally ridiculous in which to get dressed in our PT kit and fall in outside. After a frantic search for our shorts and T-shirts and regulation-issue 'Tarmac slappers' – old-fashioned black plimsolls, I believe modern-day recruits now get only the best Nike or Reebok – we were doubled down to the river. On reaching the bank, I noticed lumps of ice floating downstream, which was reassuring. We were ordered to strip naked. I didn't much fancy that. I wasn't all that bothered about my modesty but I was more than a little concerned about freezing to death in some shit-hole in Wales, but I didn't have much option other than to do as I was told.

The first recruit was ordered to get into the water. He looked terrified, poor lad, very pink and shaking, but I thought he was lucky. The watching and waiting just made it all the more stressful. The kid hesitated and was given a kindly helping hand from an NCO. Once in, and after he'd surfaced, he was ordered to do a press-up under water. He got into the press-up position and froze – no pun intended. The NCO gave him another helping hand, by dunking his head under the freezing current, after which he was able to perform the necessary water aerobics. He emerged like a drowned rat and ran to the bank to wrap himself in his green Army towel and, no doubt, have a laugh at the rest of us. After five minutes of this, it was nearly my turn. My best mate in training, Neil Handy, was in front of me and when they shouted his name he leapt into the air and started pogoing (we were both into punk music) before diving in and knocking out a quick half dozen press-ups. I thought bollocks, get it over with and I went for it, jumping in like Neil had. Almost immediately my feet went in I couldn't feel them; they kind of burned for a moment and then… nothing. I plunged my head underneath – the pain was unbearable, like someone had stuck a million pins into my skull – and I banged out three press-ups before being dragged out while the NCO screamed 'Next!'

That felt good: I had survived The Stream. Four years later, being choppered across a wintry South Atlantic, I would look down at the freezing sea and remember how cold it had been that day. Even if we ditched, it surely couldn't be *that* much worse?

It was brutal, some of our treatment, maybe some would say it teetered on the edge of torture at times. It probably wouldn't be allowed in the modern-day British Army, which is a lot softer if you believe what you read. But even then I knew it was justified. Take the anti-tank training, and the sudden rash of black eyes that ensued. They might not get away with smashing your head into a sight in the modern Army but the thinking was clear: you got one shot at trying to take out a tank. If you missed, *they'd* be taking *you* out, and a swollen eye and a bruised ego was a lot better than an incoming 125mm shell from the Soviet T72 you'd just bounced off.

Not all the recruits saw it that way, and a number of my intake of 50 quit in protest at the brutal treatment. Some lads even jacked on Day One, amazingly, and there were quite a few medical discharges. One sad case was a lad in our troop who was always at the back on runs. The

NCOs would be shouting and screaming at him to keep up and literally kicking him all the way round the course; luckily, I was a good runner and I just thought, *'Thank God that's not me'*. There wasn't a lot of sympathy knocking around back then. On one occasion, as a punishment for his slowness, we were all made to do the whole run again. One or two lads took out their frustration on this kid and beat him up, to the obvious delight of the NCOs. No-one ordered a Code Red, but it wasn't that far from *A Few Good Men,* and it was no surprise to us when there was another empty bed in our room one day. We later heard the poor lad had a serious lung condition that could have killed him. Clearly, he shouldn't have even been in the Army and it makes you wonder how he passed the medical examination.

From that initial 50, around 20 actually passed out – some literally, when they collapsed in the heat on passing out parade. Got to give them credit though, they were straight back up to attention, nose all smashed in and bleeding on the parade square Tarmac.

That passing out parade, or Goschen as it was known, busted noses and all and to the stirring tune of the British Grenadier, came in August 1979.

We all looked ever so smart in our number two-dress uniform, though many of us were wearing girls' knickers, kindly donated by the many fair maidens of Nuneaton. I believe this tradition carries on to this day. I wouldn't have minded if I had got into the pants of the lass who gave me mine; I think it was an extra pair she had in her handbag. Anyway, for the record I don't wear them now. Honest.

As an historical footnote, we also proudly wore our white lanyards, bestowed upon the Regiment after some Gunners in World War II had had the good sense to run away from a load of advancing German infantry but had failed to take the colours (field guns) with them, perhaps reasoning, and probably correctly, that this would slow them down a bit. They were labelled cowards, though I often wondered how the shiny arses (officers) would have reacted if they had been in their boots. (A lanyard, by the way, is a cord used to fire certain types of gun.) This story I discovered later was not true.

I was too young by three weeks to be posted to Germany – you had to be at least 17 years and three months old – so to mark time till I was old enough I was sent to 2nd Field Regiment, Royal Artillery, in Larkhill, Wiltshire, where I idled away the hours firing more large chunks of metal down over Salisbury plain, this time using a 105mm light gun. That was good fun: the 105mm gun was a versatile weapon, much favoured by the Commando and Para field Regiments as it could be under-slung and carried by a big helicopter, like a Sea King or Chinook, and brought into action in less than 30 seconds with a good six-man crew. Gone were the old-fashioned, dial sights that had blacked my eye so many times; these modern guns used an inertial navigational system, operated via a touch screen, and were very accurate: if you were less than 17.2ks away, and were the bad guys, you'd better duck because good Gunners could land their shells in half a badminton court at that range. I actually took a liking to this and half-wanted to stay with L Nery battery, particularly after they convinced me that being a 'Cloudpuncher' (a Rapier missile operator) was boring.

I remember we had a crash one morning on our way to the ranges when our Land Rover, pulling a 105mm gun, overturned taking a bend too quickly. There were six of us in the back with all our equipment, and I had thought we were going a bit fast, given that the roads around the ranges in Salisbury Plain are appalling, but I wasn't unduly worried. Then we started to bounce up and down a bit more; I remember watching the 105 leaving the ground and smashing back to earth and thinking, 'It shouldn't be doing that, should it?'

Next thing, the three gunners sat across from me lift up into the air and land on top of me in a mass of boots, webbing and equipment and we started rolling down the road. After half an hour or so it seemed, we came to a stop and I was dragged out with just a few cuts and bruises. A Lance Bombardier came crawling through the mud towards me and I thought, 'He must be badly hurt.'

Then he reached out and grabbed his flask. 'Thank fuck this ain't broke… brew anyone?'

He looked in shock but still retained that squaddie humour that always pulls you through the hard times.

The driver was more seriously hurt, with a few broken bones, and he had to be cut from the wreckage.

An officer wandered by and asked, 'Is there any damage to the gun?'

He didn't seem that concerned about us. Plenty more cannon-fodder where we came from. But, Heavens above, don't scratch the colours.

WORK EXPERIENCE

It was October 1979 when I was finally posted to 12 Air Defence Regiment Royal Artillery, in Dortmund, West Germany. It was one of the few times that my dad actually took an interest in me, instead of work and the pub. He came down to Luton airport with me on the train and I can remember him moaning about the cost of a pint in the airport bar; you could get a jar of Guinness at home then for about 60p and he was not impressed with being asked for £1.50 or whatever it was. I appreciated him coming down with me, but I was already a bit nervous and homesick and in a way it made it all a bit worse. But he shook my hand and wished me well and off I went to the departure lounge without looking back.

One reason I was apprehensive was I'd heard all the rumours about initiation ceremonies, a bit like before you go to senior school and you hear all the tales about having your head shoved down the toilet. As a NIG ('New Intake Gunner' or 'New In Germany'), I'd be fair game until the next bunch arrived, after which it would be my turn to make their lives a misery. It was just the pecking order: in the Army, at least in my day, if you were soft you were going to get bullied, so you had to stand up for yourself from day one. If the sweats (the senior gunners) think you will react and punch back, and you've got a decent punch on you, there's a chance they will move on to the next poor sod. Such is life. I had a bit of a head start. I wasn't a particularly hard kid but as a schoolboy I had learned to box at Pat Ryan's Catholic Boxing Club in Barrow. At Bramcote I had won the Regimental Junior Lightweight title. But I was still apprehensive.

Germany was a far cry from my safe little Cumbrian town. In fact, the whole experience was a culture shock to a 17-year-old. This was a foreign land, and in more ways than just having Deutschmarks in your pocket instead of pounds (not many, by the way; I was earning a weekly wage of around £70 a week). By and large during that period we were drunk, or at work, or both. We had a bar in our accommodation selling bottles of 'Krazy K', a very strong, locally-brewed lager, at around 60p apiece.

We'd get tanked up in the Battery bar before going down town at about 1am and getting ripped off by the Boxheads. Then we'd stagger back at about 4am, to get up again two hours later. By 8am we'd be towing things around in Land Rovers and counting down the seconds till it was time to top our alcohol reserves again.

That was pretty much how things went every day, whether you wanted to or not. To be honest, I'd have enjoyed a night off from time to time but you quickly learn to go with the flow in the Army. It's not about being an individual and that extends to every part of your life. I had to share a room with five other lads. So there was no such thing as an early night. It was a simple choice: either get thrown out of bed at four in the morning when the lads came back, or go out with them, get shit-faced and throw some other poor bastard out of his bed when you got back yourself.

The pubs were open all night, booze was flowing freely 24/7 and it was dangerous. The very first night I went down town on the ale I saw a dead body lying on the pavement, a blanket draped over it and a large pool of blood glistening darkly in the lights. People were just walking by as though it wasn't there. I was amazed at their nonchalance; even the soldiers I was with didn't give it a second glance. It wasn't until the next day that I found out the body was that of a British soldier who had been stabbed to death by some drug-crazed Turk in a fight outside a bar.

One of our locals was called the Cellar Bar; we'd often head down there to sample the local schnapps and bratties, (German bratwurst sausages) and impress the local frauleins with our wit and repartee. I remember one night we were all leaping about to the Sex Pistols and Stiff Little Fingers when a group of German bikers started a scrap with the local punks. Being helpful Brits, we went to the rescue of the punks who, on our arrival, made good their escape, leaving us in deep shit. The bikers were tooled up with pistols – we later found out they fired CS gas pellets rather than lead bullets, but we weren't to know that at the time – so we made the sort of tactical withdrawal for which the regiment became famous. Outside the club, a dozen or so shiny bikes had been neatly lined up by their proud owners; in the good hit-and-run tradition of the Long Range Desert Group we opened a few filler caps, booted the bikes over and someone threw a match at them, making our getaway in a taxi to the sanctuary of our camp as the flames leapt into the sky behind. Rule Britannia.

Thinking about it, Germany was nearly as dangerous as Northern Ireland. Leaving a bar one night on my own, I was mugged by two Germans wielding bricks. They smashed me over the head and knocked me spark out. I must have been out for a while and came to on the floor, alive but soaked in blood and with a banging headache. I flagged down a cab and went to the medical centre, where they put eight stitches in my scalp. As is routine, the medics phoned the monkeys (the military police), who took me to their HQ where I was interrogated by two over-zealous Special Investigations Branch policemen. They shined a light in my face, just like on television, and threatened to ruin my life if I didn't tell them the truth. *Who had I been with? What was I up to? Why had I been jumped?* It was all a bit bewildering – they seemed to think I'd been involved in something terribly dodgy. Soldiers hated them as everyone hated all the RMP even though they were a necessary evil. The fact was, I was the victim here and yet I was being treated as though I was the criminal. Army police don't care about technicalities like that, though: they can practically get away with murder.

Eventually they let me go. I hope the two Boxheads who mugged me spent the 10DM wisely.

There was lots of fighting with other squaddies, too, a lot of it between rival Regiments. Units called certain pubs their own and if you wandered in as a strange face they would be straight over to ask you what Regt you were with. This would usually lead to a scrap, with fists and the odd boot going in. That was fine, it went with the territory. Violence and the military go hand in hand; of course, it's supposed to be controlled aggression, so that you only fight when the brass say so, but sometimes the pressure valve blows.

Despite the ever-constant threat of getting a good kicking, I loved it. It was really exciting for a young kid from the middle of nowhere.

I was into punk music in a big way and soon got into the thriving local scene with other like-minded squaddies. I remember going AWOL one night to watch The Clash in Düsseldorf – I should have been back in camp and on guard duty but just got carried away with the booze and the music and was a day late returning. I got put on Battery Commanders Orders, a disciplinary procedure in front of a

Major who would deal with everyday occurrences like fighting and being late for duties (more serious offences would be dealt with by the Commanding Officer, a full Colonel, who could hand down a stretch in jail or court martial).

The Major, was pretty stern, telling me that the Army and punk did not mix.

He said, 'Stop being a hypocrite. You can't be a part-time anarchist. Be a soldier or get out.'

It made sense; like most squaddies, I didn't have a lot of time for Rupert's, but I did respect, and even admire, the BC in those days (though this would change, many years later). He was actually a bit of a celebrity to the lads. He was known, affectionately, as GBH because he came across as a hard bastard with a reputation for an unusual line in discipline.

Monday morning, a week or two later, I'm back before him yet again for something or other.

The charge was read out: 'Are you 24484619 Gunner McNally?'

'Yes, sir.'

'You are charged under section blah blah of the Army act 19 whatever, that you did absent yourself from your duties, contravening section blah blah of the Army act 19 blah blah. How do you plead?'

'Guilty.'

'Do you accept my award?'

His 'award' is your punishment and you haven't got a clue what it will be. He might have you mopping floors for a year, he might be going to have you shot at dawn, but if you don't accept his award you have to go before a Court Martial. So, no option really. Let's hope it's not the blindfold and the tweeting blackbirds.

'Yes, sir.'

'I charge you three days' loss of pay.'

Then he narrowed his eyes and looked at me again. 'Do you accept my award, McNally?' he repeated. 'Or would you rather step around the back?'

I'd heard tales of this before but always assumed they were embellished. I looked at him carefully: there was no hint of a smile. He was bloody serious. He was huge man and very handy, too, and I took the coward's way out

– well, I've got a white lanyard, haven't I? – And waved goodbye to the dough.

'March him out, Sergeant Major.'

From the beginning, I didn't really have the urge for promotion. More responsibilities, having to get my mates out of bed to clean the bogs. No, I was happy pissing around as a buckshee Gunner. There would be a time for seriousness, but it was not just yet.

One night me and Mel, a lad from 26 Field Regiment, pinched a Land Rover. We went tear-arsing around camp pretending that we were at Brands Hatch and we must have been spotted driving erratically as we quickly found the duty driver in hot pursuit. We out-ran him and dumped the vehicle outside the Officers Mess. The powers-that-be suspected that one of the Hooray Henries was responsible, which gave us a giggle.

On another occasion, I was nearly killed by the Boxhead civil police whilst trying to borrow a car. Me and another lad, Worm – a Cockney lad and West Ham United fanatic, who earned his nickname for his uncanny ability to worm his way out of awkward situations – had been down town pogoing and getting smashed to our hearts' content in some club or other. We were fully kitted out in punk regalia so we couldn't go through the main gate: we would have been deemed inappropriately dressed and the provost sergeant would have jailed us. This was in our minds as we wended our drunken way back to camp. We took a short-cut through a garage selling second-hand cars and Worm had the bright idea of pinching a car and doing a runner back to London. I must have been really slaughtered, because this sounded like a good plan at the time. Unfortunately, and unbeknown to us, there had been a spate of thefts from the garage and the police had the place under surveillance. As I tried the car door we were suddenly lit up like Blackpool Illuminations. We tried to leg it, the coppers shouted 'Halt' (which we ignored) and they opened fire, two rounds flying just over my head – the first time in my Army career someone had tried to shoot me. Worm found the hole in the fence; I found a German Shepherd police dog that was about to have a chunk out of my backside when its handler arrived to save me in the nick of time. I was dragged from the bushes and handcuffed and as I was thrown in to the police car one of them punched me in the face, which shocked me a bit and also sobered me up. Back at the nick, the police realised that I was a squaddie and called the Royal Military Police, who came and took a statement. I pleaded innocence: I didn't know what I'd been arrested for; I was just sneaking back into camp because of my punk clothes. Meanwhile, the Jerry cops, who obviously shouldn't have been shooting at people and punching them in the face, weren't too bothered about taking the matter further. They said I got my bloody nose when I fell while being chased, I said that I'd been alone (so once again Worm wormed his way out of a tricky situation) and the garage owner was persuaded to drop any charges.

I was dealt with by the Army, receiving a month's restriction of privileges. This meant I wasn't allowed out of camp and the Regimental Orderly Sergeant was to check I was in my bed by midnight. I got around this from time to time by paying a mate to get in my bed and pretend he was me so I could go down town and behave like a part-time anarchist.

I topped off this glorious era in my military career by going AWOL with Mick from Runcorn for two weeks. At first, we crashed at some German punk's flat, got pissed

and shagged for England – the German punkettes all
thought we sounded like Joe Strummer. When our money
ran out, we tried to make it back to the UK and got as far
as Ostende in Belgium before we were intercepted. They
roughed us up a bit, handcuffed us together in the back of a
Land Rover and we were driven all the way back to 12
Regt by squaddies from T Battery, including the guard
commander who wasn't too happy at having to give up his
Saturday collecting the Regimental waifs and strays. Mick
got a dose of the clap and I got two weeks in the
guardroom and a £200 fine. I was fortunate not to be
discharged (in more ways than one).

　　　We were always hungry and the nosh was awful. At
meal times, the Army employed Turkish labour to clear the
tables and they would slide up alongside you and snatch
your plate from underneath you, often before you'd
finished. I suppose they were doing us a favour, really, and
they probably got to take the scraps home with them. I
doubt if even the Boxhead pigs would have eaten Army
swill. To get around this, I often employed a bit of
subterfuge. If I was skint and couldn't get a pie from the
NAAFI, I'd just get into uniform, go down to the cook-

house and tell one of the slop jockeys that I'd just returned from a driving detail. He would rustle up steak and chips in between chasing the rather large rats from the kitchen and wiping the huge cockroaches from the hotplate. It wasn't exactly The Hilton, but I wasn't complaining.

Sunday afternoon tea was the most entertaining hour of the week, as the Regiment got stuck into the beer. By around 5pm, it would be on its thousandth crate of Grolsch and its members could be seen staggering to the cook-house like mustard gas victims from World War I. Some wouldn't make it and would fall by the wayside, like casualties on a battlefield. Upon reaching the food – I use the word 'food' very loosely – the proceedings would degenerate further, as hundreds of squaddies sat in rows ramming mush into their mouths like babies on their first solids. The scoff had the consistency of soggy cardboard and didn't sustain you for long; afterwards, everyone would stagger back to their crates of beer, picking up the waifs and strays on their way.

Our base was called Moore barracks and it had been a Nazi HQ during World War II. It was a cold, collection of large, Gothic-looking buildings which felt more like

Colditz than anything. The corridors were miles long – I know because, as a NIG, I had to mop them every morning – and really spooky. There were lots of rumours about the place. Some said the Nazis had hanged people from the large tree outside our room. One story had it that some builders had knocked through a wall and found a skeleton sitting on a chair where the Jerries had bricked him up years before – I thought that sort of thing went out in medieval times. There were tales of ghostly storm troopers running up and down the stairs at night and our German civilian workers wouldn't set foot in the place after dark. I've got to be honest, I didn't blame them. I used to be scared to get out of bed in the night to go to the toilet. I just felt it had an air of evil.

What I remember most about my service is the characters; the Army is full of them, far too many to mention in a book, and probably even a library. Nicknames tend to stick with you for the rest of your life. One lad joined the battery and was shown his room on the top floor in the attic. A few days later the Battery Sergeant Major asked him how he was settling in. He replied he was OK, but a bit lonely. From then on, Lonely was his name, like it or not. If it wasn't for him getting his name that way, I wouldn't remember him. There was another lad, from up north somewhere. He was a total half-bake. He left his locker open and lost all of his kit except for one mess tin. He didn't even know how to fasten his bootlaces properly. He went AWOL and was apparently settling in nicely in the less salubrious parts of Amsterdam before they caught him and returned him to camp. Where he saluted the BSM after calling him 'Corporal'. I think he got away with it, pretty much, and it was rumoured that his father was someone who knew someone, which explains both that and why he was allowed to join up in the first place.

I suppose I was lucky I was just 'Mack' throughout my service.

Six months in and I'd gone from being a punk to being a skinhead, with my hair so closely-cropped it was like a chin after one day's growth. Me and my mates had been banned by the Regimental Sergeant Major (or God, to give him his correct title) from having excessively short haircuts, but we'd decided to chance it anyway. The RSM decided that since we had disobeyed him he would make an example of us so he made us wear our tin helmets, which were painted a fetching T Battery blue, without the inner liner. That's very uncomfortable, believe me. But we relished this and wouldn't be seen without them – in the cook-house, in the NAAFI, the shower, and even in bed. Needless to say, this punishment didn't work; we turned his humiliation of us into a joke.

It was about this time that the Soviets invaded Afghanistan. As a young squaddie, this certainly gave me pause for thought; if nothing else, it made me realise that, stuck in Germany, I was much too close to the Red Army for comfort. Gunner McNally and his oppos would be the first line of defence in any invasion of the west and that didn't fill me with the joys of spring. Do you know how many blokes they had? The odds would have been about five million to one in their favour.

To be fair, despite this I didn't really think that I would ever end up fighting a real war with live missiles and dead bodies, but we still practiced, just in case. After the invasion, training was stepped up and became almost continuous. Range days for rifle practice blended into hours of physical activity and then endless nuclear, biological and chemical warfare training. This was no fun at all; the NBC threat was seen as a terrifying reality, and fighting in a 'noddy suit' was definitely not my idea of a good time.

I remember one exercise, called 'Active Edge'. This was supposed to test how ready we were to repel a Soviet-led invasion of West Germany (answer: not very). The whole thing was a bit of a farce from start to finish.

For starters, everybody seemed to know that Active Edge would be called sometime on Saturday night. The clues were there for all to see: all the pads (married personnel, who normally live in married quarters) were told they'd be sleeping in our block in their green kit, we were all confined to camp and alcohol was (supposedly) strictly prohibited. So we'd all lie there in bed, waiting for the balloon to go up. Then, bugger me, at 0200 hrs, the call would go out: *Active Edge.*

We'd all leg it to the Gun Park, jump in the wagons and trundle away into the woods. About an hour and a half later, we would deploy our Rapier missiles.

The CO would pick one lucky Battery and inspect its equipment. Sometimes you would have to show your sewing kit (Housewife) or underpants, or socks, or toothbrush.

After 24 hours, we would receive orders to cease firing (though no actual firing had occurred – we had dummy missiles on the launcher). At breakneck speed, we would pack everything up and race back to camp. On our return, every little piece of equipment, down to the last spanner, had to be cleaned and put back in the stores. The vehicles were steam-cleaned and then totally repainted green and brown. This was a massive pain in the backside at the time though; looking back I can obviously see the reasoning: it means that your equipment, which you will rely on to keep you and your mates alive in wartime, is in serviceable condition. At the time, though, it just delayed the serious business of getting drunk again.

Meanwhile, the Soviets would be monitoring our movements. You can just imagine their radio chatter: 'Dmitri… something is occurring in West Germany.'

'Don't panic, Igor. It's only 12 Regt on *Active Edge* again.'

If I sound cynical, I probably was. I understand you need to go through the motions sometimes, just practising what goes where and when. But I didn't think the Russians were likely to drop us a line telling us that they planned to invade next weekend. Or maybe I'm wrong. Maybe the Warsaw pact had some sort of agreement with NATO that they wouldn't attack us on New Year's Eve, when almost the whole of the British Army of the Rhine, in common with the rest of Western Europe, was completely comatose?

After all the aggro in Germany, I was quite pleased to hear in May 1981 that we were going home to a quiet little base in the UK, at Kirton Lindsey. This was a little village about eight miles away from Scunthorpe; if you had been passing through, you would have been amazed to discover that there was a whole Regiment concealed somewhere nearby.

They loved our money in the local pub, but that's where the romance ended. The locals were a bit strange: you wouldn't have been at all surprised to find them all running around the village green naked, with burning crosses, chanting to Satan. Then again, there were some strange characters in our mob, too.

Wednesday afternoon was sports afternoon, and we soon got onto a good thing. We were allowed to go swimming in the town of Brig, unsupervised. We'd get our swimming togs, and green Army towel and set off but the nearest we got to water was downing a beer in the pub.

One afternoon, me and my mate Eddie 'Scouse' Denmark were thumbing it back to camp, as we'd spent up. I noticed a dead hare in the road, picked it up and proceeded to chase Scouse down the road with the maggot-ridden carcass, when a car stopped just ahead of us.

'We're in luck,' I shouted and we both ran over to the car. Oops! An officer was at the wheel. I dropped the hare. The Officer stuck his head out of the window.

'I presume you're going to Kirton.'

'Yes, sir.'

'Jump in, then.'

Funnily, he never said more than a dozen words. He turned out to be the 2nd in command of 12 Regiment; I wonder how he knew we were squaddies?

The atmosphere was more like a university campus than an Army barracks. One bonfire night, Scouse and I had got hold of some fireworks. Pyrotechnics and young soldiers don't go together: we proceeded to launch an assault on the block. We went around the back of T

Battery accommodation, with a snapped-off fluorescent light tube containing a large rocket. I put the tube on my shoulder like an RPG7, Scouse lit the fuse and – whoosh!...off it went through an open window, exploding spectacularly inside. I suppose it could have been quite dangerous, but nobody was hurt. It was a good job we didn't get caught as we were on fire picket at the time; it was our duty to make sure there was no risk of fire around the camp and to fight it with the old-fashioned tender until the local town brigade turns up.

We quickly got into a routine. Start work Monday morning at 0800 hrs, finish work Friday afternoon 1630 hrs and after a shower, a shave and a few jars in the NAAFI bar, I'd be on the train home to Dalton in time for last orders and a pint of mild in The Newton pub. It was all pretty run-of-the-mill military life – mostly lots of polishing, sweeping, cleaning, and such. Our RSM at this time was an Irish gentleman who was always good for a laugh.

'You, yes you, come here!' he'd scream at the top of his voice, pointing his pace stick at me like some deadly sabre.

I'd smartly march up to him and come to attention.

'If you are walking past a tree, and you see a leaf that even *looks* as if it's just about to fall off, I want you to pick it off and put it in your pocket.'

'Yes, sir.'

'Carry on. And get a haircut.'

As I marched away, he would notice that my hair was more than short enough already and change his order. 'A neck shave will do.'

'Yes, sir,' as I march away, busting a gut laughing.

We went on the odd exercise to places like Otterburn ranges, in Northumberland the North East of England, where we would practice tracking A10 Thunderbolt tank buster jets of the US Air Force. I happily once drove a Land Rover the whole way to Denmark, too, towing thousands of pounds-worth of missile unit with me, which wasn't bad for a lad without a driving licence. Well, have you ever seen a civvie police stop an Army convoy? We spent two weeks camped in a field, getting slaughtered and generally having a good time before the war game started. That meant about three days trying to look like professional soldiers, moving from one location near a pig farm to another location near another pig farm. At the end of it all, just for a change, the Battery went on the razzle in Copenhagen. Great for a game of 'Spot The Squaddie': everyone was a skinhead and dressed in tee-shirt, jeans and desert wellies, and had a black bin-liner full of cheap beer bought earlier from the Battery Bar thrown over the shoulder, us Brits are canny with our money you know.

The main event of the trip was having a scrap with a load of Belgian Paratroopers in a fountain – nothing too serious, just a few black eyes and bloody noses – and a Scouse Bombardier being ejected from a brothel, stark bollock-naked and with a lump on his head after being hit with a vacuum cleaner for good measure. I never found out why he was thrown out – he probably thought he hadn't got his money's worth. I had a tattoo done on my right wrist: 'A-Pos', my blood group, which was all I could afford, a lad pinched a car and crashed and then we returned home to our little Trumpton Town Hamlet.

Another exercise found us in Germany, at Saltau Ranges near Hamburg. After we'd finished playing soldiers, we headed into town to visit the infamous Reeperbahn, home of die sündige meile (the sinful mile), a messy and well-named hotchpotch of bars, brothels and peep shows where we all got pleasantly shit-faced and generally misbehaved ourselves.

Before we knew it, time had caught up with us and it was time to go back to camp. It was only midnight and the place was just coming alive, so we were a bit pissed off as we clambered into the big olive green Army taxi at the pick-up point. I wasn't looking forward to the 30 mile trip back, so I looked at Scouse. 'I bet you don't have the balls to jump off the wagon.' I said.

'You first,' he said, so I did. I didn't think he'd follow but he did and we ran off into the night, a chorus of 'You dickheads are in the shit now!' from our comrades ringing in our ears.

Like we cared; the night was young. We knew we were in for a bollocking, but you only live once. After drinking ourselves nearly sober on beer and Schnapps, we collapsed asleep in a shop doorway and woke up to a 5am sky and lots of shouting and arguing from the pizza shop next door. Suddenly, a Turkish guy came running out, followed by a big German guy. They were rowing and squaring up to one another, jostling a bit, and as we watched the German pulled out a pistol and shot the Turk in the chest at point blank range. Then he just went back inside like it was nothing, leaving the injured man groaning in a pool of blood.

'Fucking hell, Scouse,' I said. 'Did you see that?'

As if he could have missed it.

'Yep,' said Scouse. 'Let's fuck off before the bizzies arrive.'

We were up and gone in a matter of moments. Amazingly, we didn't really talk about the shooting we had just witnessed, which shows how desensitised to violence Army life makes you. I don't know if the guy died and at the time I didn't give a toss one way or the other.

We discussed stealing a car to get back to camp – well, we were desperate – but as it was getting light we binned the idea. Just as well, given that we were both still steaming and would almost certainly have crashed and killed ourselves or someone else.

We found the railway station and found we had enough small change left to buy tickets half way to Saltau, which was better than nothing. After cadging 1DM to buy

STILL WATCHING MEN BURN

a cup of tea, we fell asleep on the train and were kicked awake by the German guard when we got to our destination, a tiny one-horse station in the middle of nowhere.

Luckily there was a map on the station wall and it had Saltau marked on it, so we tried to orientate ourselves. Map-reading was never a strong point of either of us – we tended to travel on exercise by road, and our sergeant always had the map – but we came up with a plan which took us in roughly the right direction and set off on a ten mile walk. It was coming up to noon, now, and we knew we were in trouble, but we had a good laugh about it and ambled through the forest in no great rush. A bollocking can always wait, in my book.

Eventually, two or three hours later, we made out the shape of the camp in the distance and started to work on our excuses.

Everyone was busy with their duties when we emerged from the woods like two desperado fugitives, unshaven and in our scruffy civvie clothes. First a few of our mates saw us and started giggling; then an NCO walked by. 'Where the fuck have you two clowns been?'

he shouted. 'You'd better go and report to the BSM… and fucking double there!'

We ran, as requested, and found ourselves in front of the BSM a few moments later, feet slammed together, trying to look as sheepish and sorry as possible.

'Well if it isn't Gunners McNally and Denmark,' he said. 'So glad you could both join us this morning.'

We stared straight ahead at attention and said nothing.

'Why the fuck did you both miss the transport last night? I have been told that you were both on the Bedford and then jumped off?'

'Yes Sir,' I said.

'Yes Sir,' said Scouse.

'Fucking *'Yes Sir'*… is that all you idiots can say?'

'Sir, I can explain Sir,' I said.

'Please do enlighten me, McNally.'

'Sir I got back to the transport in good time and climbed aboard ready to go back to camp, when I suddenly realised that I had left my jacket in the last bar I'd been in. Sir, realising that my ID card was in the jacket I panicked and went back for it, Sir.'

'And I suppose you just went with him to hold his hand, Denmark?'

'Yes Sir, I thought it best I went with him.'

'Did you now?'

'Yes Sir.'

'You realise that you are both in serious trouble don't you?'

'Yes Sir.' In unison.

The BSM was tapping his stick on his table and looking at us both like he was planning the best way to execute us. Then he stood bolt upright.

'Right, you two morons. You've got five minutes to sort your shit out, and then I want you washed, shaved and in uniform to report to the cookhouse for a day's Dixie Bashing (Dish Washing). And don't think for a minute that I believed that cock and bull story of yours.'

'Sir!' we both screamed, and made for the door before he changed his mind.

'One more thing,' he said. 'Did you get your leg over?'

'Sir!'

'Now get out!'

'Sir'

We were gone, let off very lightly. The BSM was a good guy; he'd been a Gunner once and I think he liked a soldier with a bit of character.

I ought to point out, by the way, that although I was often getting into scrapes, I took my soldiering seriously. My reports from that time talk about a conscientious and popular soldier with above average ability at aspects of my work. Which I think was fair. I was one of the fittest soldiers in the Regiment along with Scouse, always come in first or the first three of a BFT (Basic Fitness Test), member of the boxing team and cross country team, if I was ever called to go to War I was ready.

Our Dixie Bashing over, we headed back to Kirton where we got on with the serious business of sweeping the leaves, painting the kerb stones black and white and polishing the brasses on RHQ.

I got myself fixed up with a local girl called Carole that I met in Tiffany's the local nightclub in sunny Scunnie by pretending that I was a civilian contractor. When I'd first chatted her up, she'd only let me buy her a drink as long as I wasn't 'one of those bloody squaddies from Kirton.'

'No way,' I said. 'Can't stand the bullshit, wouldn't last five minutes in the Army.'

I carried on with this sham for a few weeks but it couldn't last, especially when squaddies kept walking past, saying 'All right Mack?'

'How do they know you?'

'Oh, I've been doing a bit of brickie work up at the camp.'

The penny wasn't far off dropping so I admitted what I was in the end; luckily, by this time she seemed to fancy me and had started asking me home for tea.

I sometimes think I might have ended up married to Carole, if it wasn't for some small, sheep-infested island in the South Atlantic getting invaded.

ALL AT SEA

Army life in our sleepy little village was about to be turned upside down by events taking place 8,000 miles away in the icy waters off an island nobody had even heard of.

Everybody was in a fairly jovial mood at the time because we were about to go on Easter block leave for a fortnight. It was a particularly happy time for me, as I was taking Carole home to Dalton to meet my Mam and dad.

They never did meet get to her, sadly.

The initial warning was given at 10.45hrs, Friday 2nd April 1982, two hours before we were officially off on leave, which left us all well hacked-off. No-one was going anywhere: guys in other units who had actually gone home had been called as soon as they got there and ordered to do an about-turn and set off back to camp. It was a ball-ache but it was all part and parcel of being a professional soldier: the Army owned us, and that was that.

The mood improved once we found out what the crack was. Some Argentineans had apparently invaded an island somewhere off the coast of Scotland, and we all got very excited about the thought of going up there and giving the cheeky bastards a good kicking. The buzz carried on even after some bright spark took the time to look at a map.

We started the huge task of preparing the whole Battery for the real McCoy. It was something we trained for, but somehow – in my day, at least – didn't quite think you'd ever do. I'd always been a fairly keen soldier underneath it all, and now I upped my focus still further, really getting stuck in. As T Battery was part of the Army's Ace Mobile Force, we were on standby to be sent to any trouble spots around the world on very short notice. That meant we had first dibs on any working equipment, so all our duff bits of kit, and we had a lot of them, were exchanged with our sister Battery, 58 Eyres. They were left with virtually nothing that worked. Good job no-one told the Soviets that. Faulty kit doesn't matter too much if you're on exercise, as nobody's really going to get hurt. I wish I had a pound for the times I've heard, 'Ah well, we'll be going home tomorrow, lads… we live to play another day.' But war is different: you usually only get one chance, and I shudder to think what would have happened if 58 Bty had been needed for an operational tour after we left. This woeful lack of equipment really was a sad state of affairs, and one which hasn't improved, given all the stories of lads being deployed to Iraq and Afghanistan with no body armour and not enough rounds and faulty radios.

Unbelievably, given that the Army is as bureaucratic and lethargic as any major government institution, we were ready to go and kick some Latin American arses by 1800 hrs on Saturday 3rd April 1982.

I gave Carole a quick phone call, a minute or two, tops. She would probably have appreciated a little more effort on my part but I was full of nervous excitement about the prospect of going to war and relationships were not high on my list of priorities.

And then we were on the road. It took us sixteen hours on a shagged-out old Army bus to get from Kirton to the docks in Plymouth Devon, but we loved every minute. We felt like heroes already, as news had leaked out to the media by now and Joe Public had a good idea where we were going. All the way down, motorists were beeping their horns and Union Jacks appeared from everywhere to wave us on our way. It made me feel really proud for once in my life: we all got quite carried away by the patriotism of the people, and all the flag waving and cheering, and I had a lump in my throat all the way down there. But, like most people, if I'd had to put my wages on it I'd have said it would all turn out to be a false alarm, and that as soon as we arrived in Plymouth the Argies would bottle it and sod off home for a corned beef buttie.

The ship in which we were going to sail half way around the world was a grey, flat-bottomed old rust bucket called the RFA (Royal Fleet Auxiliary) *Sir Geraint*. (The RFA is a civilian-manned fleet owned by the MOD whose main task is to resupply the warships of the Royal Navy at sea so they can remain operational while away from base, but it also provides secure sea transport for Army units and their equipment.) The *Sir Geraint* reminded me of the sort of old-fashioned tub you saw on the telly when the US Marines were about to invade some Pacific island crawling with Japs. She didn't exactly fill me with confidence but as it turned out she was a trusty old thing and was one of the very few that didn't take a direct hit. Mind you, I almost missed the boat altogether. On the last day of shore leave in Plymouth, I was nearly run over by a taxi whilst looking for a barbers shop. I had to look smart for my last session in the local hostelries of Union Street. I had many a free pint bought for me that night by the many back-slappers and armchair warriors, and I was grateful for every one I downed.

Our leader, GBH, left us at Plymouth so he could sail south on *HMS Fearless* to co-ordinate our role in the bigger picture of things with the other senior officers. We were now part of 3rd Commando Brigade and would be cruising down with 79 Bty of 29 Commando Regt, RA, and a key element of 3 Commando Brigade. These boys were all Commando-qualified and trained in Arctic warfare, helicopter and amphibious assault and, in many cases, parachute assault too. They were also very fine gunners. They knew us as 'crap hats', shortened to just 'hat'. If you don't wear a red (Parachute Regiment) or green (Royal Marines) beret in the British armed forces you are known as a crap hat (unless you wear the beige-coloured one of the SAS). But we hats do have our moments, as we'll see later on.

The long process of loading all the stores on board began. It won't surprise you to read that the only thing we ever seemed to load was boxes of beer, like a line of khaki-clad alcoholic ants filling their nest. Well, it was going to be a long journey.

We finally set sail on Tuesday 6th April 1982.

Later, when I came back home, I remember watching TV pictures of the Paras sailing off into the horizon on the luxury liner, Canberra, with thousands of people waving and women flashing their boobs. The Scots Guards went in style, too, on the QE2. Our departure was rather more low-key: it was just getting dark when we slipped quietly away, with about 10 dock workers standing watching us, their hands in their pockets, probably thinking 'I wonder where all those dozy pillocks are off to?'

Some of the lads started throwing coins to them; I don't know if it's some sort of naval tradition but I remember thinking it should have been the other way around.

Still, who gave a toss? I wasn't really going to war, was I?

As we didn't think it would end up in a live-firing exercise, we were looking forward to a little cruise. But it wasn't exactly five star stuff: in fact, it was horribly cramped on board, with two-fully equipped Batteries vying for what little space there was. The *Sir Geraint* could carry 340 troops comfortably but there were well over 500 lads and crew aboard, together with all our stores. There were about 50 men per mess deck and practically no space at all for personal items, apart from essentials like your washing and shaving gear, your PT kit and a change of uniform, and a few porn mags. It wasn't much fun. The only privacy you got was when you hung your green Army towel down from the bunk above at night. By the way, it's not true about sending you blind, but you do end up with a sore wrist.

It was important to stop boredom setting in, because we all know what the Devil does with idle hands, so a training programme was quickly worked out. As T Bty were not trained to fight in Arctic conditions, and since it was going to be bloody cold where we were headed, we relied on our Commando buddies of 79 Bty to bring us up to date. They taught us how to dig a snow hole, which isn't as easy as it sounds, and the basic signs of hypothermia and how to treat it. They tried to teach us Morse code – the old dot-dot dash-dash malarkey – which gives you some idea of how tedious it got. In return, we were able to help them with aircraft recognition, part of the anti-aircraft gunner's trade. In theory, our Rapiers physically couldn't engage friendly planes and choppers because of the automatic IFF (Identification Friend or Foe) system. In practice, it is obviously very important to be able to identify aircraft visually too. It's probably a lot more sophisticated now but back then our IFF system worked by interrogating approaching aircraft with radio signals, which were sequences of coded numbers. If the target was 'friendly' it would recognise the code and send back the correct friendly response, and the missiles would relax. If the response didn't arrive the system would assume it was a 'foe' and it would be engaged.

However, the equipment wasn't fool- proof by any means, and the opportunities for blue-on-blue (friendly fire) incidents were ever-present, so it was vitally important that we were able to recognise everything in the air with the naked eye so as to minimise the risk. In the past, as part of BAOR, we had all learned to identify Soviet aircraft, which were all known to us by NATO code-names (fighters like Fishbeds, Floggers, Fitters, helicopters like

Hind, Hip and Halo). But the Argies would be trying to kill us in aircraft that would previously have been friendlies: the French Mirage and its Dagger variant, the American A4 Sky Hawk, their own Pucara (they had nearly 150 of these) and the Italian Aermacchi MB339. Their main helicopter was the US Jet Ranger and they were also potentially going to be transporting men and materiel in the C130 Hercules and Chinook choppers, both of which were used by our own armed forces too. The potential for shit and fan colliding with each other in a catastrophic way was obvious, so a lot of homework had to be done. As they say: know your enemy.

The crew of the *Geraint* were mainly Hong Kong Chinese, and there wasn't much these little fellows couldn't do. They cooked the meals, ran the laundry, would operate the anti-aircraft guns and fight fires if we were hit and they even cut our hair. Not with clippers, mind you, but the old way, with scissors and a cut-throat.

The Chinese are very proud and loyal people, much like the Gurkhas, and you couldn't help liking them, but not everyone treated them with maximum respect. One morning, early in the trip, we were lined up for breakfast when one of our lads shouted over, 'What's this shite, then?'

This is a phrase heard every day in Army cook-houses round the world.

The difference is, our slop-jockeys were used to being insulted and relished giving it back to you in spades; the Chinese were not so well-rounded. The gentleman behind the counter made his feelings quite clear by chasing the terrified squaddie around the ship with a meat cleaver until he cornered the lad in the heads (the naval word for 'bogs'), where he locked himself in and refused to come out again until the coast was clear. After that there was a lot more 'please' and 'thank you' flying around.

One afternoon, we had to move a load of sacks of potatoes from above decks down to the galley. Some of the bags burst open and there were lots of loose spuds rolling about. I picked one of the biggest I could find and threw it as hard as I could at the back of the head of a Chinese sailor, quickly looking at the floor as if I hadn't seen anything. The sailor let out a scream and spun round, looking accusingly at Scouse, who frantically pleaded his innocence while we all fell about wetting ourselves and slipping around in the crushed-up potato.

Once we'd sailed away from UK waters, we could go up on deck. I had broken something of a seafaring tradition in our family by joining the Army. My Dad had wanted to me to join the Navy, as his father had been a ship's Captain on the old SS White Star Line. As a fifteen-year-old schoolboy, I had visited HMS Leander when it came to Barrow. It was enjoyable enough looking around, and a matelot doing his recruitment bit had walked over and asked me if I was joining the Navy when I left school.

My mind was already made up. 'No,' I said, proudly. 'I'm joining the Army.'

He looked at me in disgust and said, 'You don't want to do that, son, they'll send you to Northern Ireland. People will be shooting at you, and all sorts. Join a nice, safe profession and see the world.'

Tell that to the lads on the *Sheffield*, the *Coventry* and the *Antelope*, mate.

Anyway, my granddad would have been proud of me now. I probably spent more time at sea than some sailors do and I even got to grips with the lingo. There's the heads, of course, and then the floor is the 'deck', the walls are 'bulkheads', the back is the 'stern' and left and right are port and starboard. I also quickly became acquainted with the tedious monotony of life at sea. Every day was the same. Join the queue for the heads, wash and shave, stow your maggot (sleeping bag) and clean the mess deck ready for the Captain's rounds, where the Captain of the ship inspects and makes sure everything is ship shape. You were herded from port to starboard, fore to aft, where everyone was trying to get their little bit of deck nice and shiny for the skipper.

Topside there was nothing to see for miles and miles: just water, and the odd seabird, and then the horizon curving away to nothing. It felt very lonely: we were in our own little cocoon, our own small boat sailing down with no-one to keep us company. We had no idea of the scale of the task force steaming down with us, just out of sight beyond the curvature of the earth.

As this was still the very early stage of 'Operation Corporate', we were all still in a fairly happy and relaxed state of mind; this was just a show of strength by Maggie Thatcher, a bit of sabre-rattling. The Argies were just bluffing and would bottle it and withdraw to the mainland before we got halfway down there. Even better, with no pubs to spend our cash in, it was a good way of saving some beer money before we turned round for home and started our Easter leave again.

The further we went, the worse the weather; the seas became mountainous and the inevitable epidemic of seasickness broke out. I think we were in the Bay of Biscay when it really kicked in. Seasickness sounds like a minor inconvenience but anyone who has suffered it badly will know what I mean when I say I just wanted to curl up and die. Sadly, we had a war to train for, so we were given some injections that seemed to make it even worse and just got on with it (puking up everywhere, I mean).

I think the first thing that made us concentrate our minds a little was when a sergeant came round dishing out Army wills for us to fill in one afternoon. I don't know what our Mam would have done with all my worldly possessions (which amounted to one carrier bag-full of non-green kit), but she would have got them anyway. Filling in the form brought it home to me that I could actually be going to war here; in a month or two, people I hadn't even met might be trying to kill me, and they might even succeed. It gave a lot of the other guys a few moments' thought, too, but the general consensus was that it was fine: it was why we signed on the dotted line.

We were trying hard to keep morale up, something which is important to all soldiers but is even more so for units like ours. A Rapier Battery has its own peculiar role within the Royal Artillery. Conventional gun Batteries consist of six guns, all grouped together in close proximity in order that they can concentrate their fire and blow the hell out of the bad guys before our infantry can close and take a given piece of ground. Unlike the guns, Rapiers are essentially defensive weapons and so are air-lifted to protect a variety of potential targets, such as ground troops, ammo dumps, HQs and bridges. You can find yourself some distance, even miles, from the other eleven fire units in your Battery. This means a smaller group of blokes who mix together more of the time; each system was manned by seven men, a Sergeant, a Bombardier, a Lance-Bombardier and four Gunners and we would be in each other's pockets all day, every day. We really had to get along with each other, to trust each other with our lives, even if we hated each other's guts, in order to stay alive and get the job done. Assuming the Argentineans stood fast, where we were going, there wouldn't be an umpire saying 'You lie down, you're dead' as they do on exercise. The parade-ground bullshit was out of the window. Our detachment got on OK, as it happened. We weren't particularly close back in the barracks, but we all pulled together and worked as a team during the journey south.

One thing that did worry us during the voyage was the bashing around the Rapiers had taken when they were brought aboard. They'd been loaded with all the loving care you associate with normal Army loading – i.e. none – and now, to add insult to injury, they were down below in the Tank Deck, jigging around and getting nicely damp in the salt air. At least one of the launchers was damaged whilst being loaded, which was not a good start. It sounds ridiculous: we were on our way to fight a war, and the kit ought to have been be able to take a bit of punishment. But Rapier was never designed to travel 8,000 miles across the rolling Atlantic in a flat-bottomed boat. It was designed to travel on the roads and fields of western Europe, a Land Rover towing the launcher, followed by a second Land

Rover, known as a detachment support vehicle, carrying the rest of the equipment, tracker and crew. It was a notoriously sensitive bit of kit, with lots of things that could go wrong, and this treatment was a major concern. The motion of the ship wasn't our only worry. Unlike home, the Falklands weren't known for its miles of tarmac, gentle meadow and well-made Teutonic forest tracks. It was basically a craggy hill jutting up out of the waves and we would be relying on Sea King helicopters to lug us around. That meant more jolting and bashing for the Rapiers.

Mind you, the truth was that nobody really knew how the equipment would work in a combat situation anyway. A field gun can be fired every day, whereas – missiles being expensive things – Rapier Regiments were limited to live-firing once a year, at Benbecula in the Outer Hebrides. It didn't get much more exciting than a day up there: you aimed at a long, metal cylinder known as a 'Rushton' which was towed behind a Canberra bomber. It was extremely hard to actually get a hit; the target was only about 10 feet long, much smaller than an aircraft, and it was a couple of miles away and travelling at around 400 knots. If you did manage to hit the bloody thing, which was either a total fluke or meant you were the direct descendant of William Tell (I never did), you got a tee shirt and a crate of beer. On the plus side, at least it didn't fire back. The rest of the time, we had used a simulator, practising tracking and engaging targets on film footage. This was OK, but to be honest some of today's modern arcade games are a lot more realistic and they take more skill, too.

This lack of proper practice was ridiculous, really. Each missile cost something like fifteen grand and it was simply a matter of saving money. But if you weigh that against the cost of losing a ship or a fighter to an enemy aircraft missed by a guy who's never been trained properly, it sounds like a false economy to me. (The craziest thing of all was that it was possible for a Rapier operator *never* to live-fire. You could sign up for as few as three years, which meant three opportunities. You only had to be otherwise engaged at the relevant times and that was your chance gone. In fact, there was a lad in our Battery who, once posted from depot, didn't even fire a rifle. He was very much into sport, and spent his career playing football, cricket and hockey, which must have been nice for him. I believe he is now a PT instructor in the Birmingham area.) All that said, even live firing had a crucial missing element – fear. The only real way to judge how a Rapier operator will react when he's crapping in his combats would be to put a loaded gun to his head and threaten to blow it off if he didn't hit the target, and I couldn't see that being introduced any day soon, not even by the old Scots Drill Sergeant Major from Bramcote.

From a day or so out of Plymouth, the stink of sweat filled the *Sir Geraint* all day long. Ships can only carry a limited amount of fresh water, and with several hundred squaddies on board it had to be rationed. This meant standing in the shower, turning the water on, getting slightly wet, turning the water off, soaping, turning the water back on for five seconds and rinsing. What I would have given to sit in the bottom with the shower full on, supping a bottle of chilled Newcastle Brown Ale, (or 'Dog', as it is known in Cumbria).

At night, everyone congregated in the canteen and we all queued up to buy our rations of five cans of beer. It used to amaze me how some people could get blind drunk on five cans; however, where there's a thirsty squaddie, there's a way (usually a way involving theft or bribery). There was a good atmosphere, with lots of card games going on. We invented a horse-racing game, too. Tables were joined together and a cloth racecourse track was laid out. There were several wooden horses a punter could bid for. Four or five horses were placed at the start and then a die would be rolled. If the die came up seven, then the chosen horse would move along seven places, and so on until one horse eventually won. Vast quantities of money were won and lost on this game every night.

On the whole, things were good-humoured, considering that hats and cabbage heads were mixing together with lots of booze swilling around to help things develop. It would have been a different tale if it had been Paras and Commandos sharing the same boat: light the blue touch paper, stand back and wait for the riot.

There was one serious incident, when two huge RA Commandos had a row with a Sergeant Major and thought it would be a good idea to throw him in the sea to find out if he could swim back to Britain. They were arrested and charged with mutiny and eventually flown back to the UK

to sit out the rest of the war in the MCTC (the Military
Corrective Training Centre, or jail, in Colchester).

Just to get us really frustrated, we were shown porno
films most nights. I'd sit with my legs crossed, bladder
busting, waiting for the end, to avoid the jeers of 'Oi,
wanker, where are you going, you dirty bastard?' Some
nights, I'd sit watching the films, can of beer in hand, and
my own personal barber, who had his own shop in Hong
Kong, giving me a skinhead.

By now, we'd been at sea several weeks and as we
headed towards the equator the weather was getting warm;
when you could get up on deck, and if you could put
everything out of your mind, it did begin to feel like a
cruise in the sunshine. Sunbathing was the order of the day,
but you had to be careful not to get burned; your body
belonged to the Army and you weren't allowed to damage
it. If we did, you were fined several days' pay, depending
on the severity of the burn. If several of you got burned on
your backs you were made to leap-frog over one another as
a deterrent.

Walkmans and tapes were like gold dust, as were
radios, which helped us to keep up to date with the news

and world cup football results on the BBC World Service. It wasn't exactly encouraged: the officers didn't really want us to know too much about the outside world, or what was going on back home; the idea was to keep our minds firmly set on the task ahead and avoid homesickness.

We were looking forward to stopping at our halfway point, the Ascension Islands. This is a British territory 1,000 miles from the west coast of Africa, some 4,250 miles from the UK and around 3,800 miles from Port Stanley. Having never heard of the place before, and being a Standard Issue 19-year-old lad, I had conjured up images of white sands and palm trees, the local female natives waiting to greet us, swaying gently in their grass skirts and flower garlands, and beckoning to us seductively.

I was to be sadly disappointed. There wasn't a woman in sight and, far from being a tropical paradise; the island was a barren lump of volcanic rock in the middle of nowhere. It's basically a mountain which ascends around 3,000ft into the sky – hence the name. It was an ugly, depressing place; apparently, NASA tested the moon buggy there due to the similarity of its terrain with that of the moon.

The high point of our visit was standing on deck watching shoals of piranha-like fish eating the contents of our heads as it was flushed out into the sea. We took it in turns: 'This time, you go to the bog, and I'll watch.' If pushed, the average soldier could find pointless amusement on the inside of a ping-pong ball.

As well as resupplying us and providing an opportunity for maintenance, the idea was that we would do a bit of a mini-rehearsal – beach landings and invasion-type things. The Rapier crews were looking forward to some live firing of our missiles, which would have been a valuable exercise, a chance to feel solid ground beneath your feet and get your eye back in. But for whatever reason – we were never told why – this didn't happen. Instead, we had to make do with practising limited fly-offs, getting used to working with the choppers who would be lifting the kit. One useful thing we learned from this was that we could stow the optical trackers in the back of one-ton Land Rovers whilst in transit, which meant tracker and Rover went in one lift instead of two, saving valuable time. Unfortunately, we worked this out only after we'd heaved and sweated them up from the hold to the stern helicopter pad.

We were on our way almost before we had stopped but no-one was all that disappointed when we set back off on our life on the ocean wave. The politicians, safe in their oak-panelled offices in London, were keen that we continued our progress and got to grips with the Argies as quickly as possible, and we felt the same way.

The atmosphere aboard ship changed now, though. As we entered May, the tension on board was increasing every day. The mess deck seemed to get smaller; we were getting sick of living like sardines, and arguments broke out over trivial things. There was a noticeable step-up of training. We ran around the deck of the boat for mile after bloody mile of monotonous sameness, and sweated buckets in PT sessions on the helicopter pad in the blazing sun under the unforgiving gaze of our PTIs (Physical Training Instructors). We went over weapons skills, first aid and aircraft recognition again and again and again. We covered the rules of the Geneva Convention – how to treat prisoners and what to do if we were captured… the old name, rank and number routine. We did this with the usual

STILL WATCHING MEN BURN

squaddie sense of humour: 'I'm going to tell them my Regiment as well. They'll probably have worn the sheep out by now, and we'll be next if we don't.'

At the back of my mind, a lingering feeling, that maybe this was all headed for proper fisticuffs after all, was getting stronger and stronger. And as we chugged slowly south, plenty of the other guys seemed to be thinking the same thing. By now, South Georgia had been re-taken from the scrap metal merchants and the Argentine Marines and two Vulcan bombers had dropped a total of nine tons of explosives on the runway at Port Stanley, the Falklands' capital and now the main Argentinean base. They caused only limited damage and the Argies continued to use the runway right up to the end of the war. (The mission sounds a bit like a failure: all that way from England – the world's longest-ever bombing mission at the time – and they miss. The truth was it was a strategic success, because it made the Argies sit up and take notice; if we could hit them there, we could hit them on their mainland. They withdrew their fighters from the airfield to protect their home bases and this was to reduce the effectiveness of their air force during the conflict.)

At 1600 hrs on the 2nd May came one of the major incidents of the war, when *HMS Conqueror*, a Royal Navy submarine, attacked the Argentine flagship, *General Belgrano*. The *Conqueror* fired a pair of torpedoes into the ageing battleship and sank her, killing 300 sailors in the process and leaving a further 700-odd survivors in the freezing South Atlantic waters, where a number of them died from their injuries or exposure before most were picked up.

To some people, this was a very controversial engagement – infamously celebrated by *The Sun* with the headline 'Gotcha!' Maggie had imposed a 200-mile total exclusion zone around the Falklands and authorised the Royal Navy to destroy Argentinean ships found within that area. But the *Belgrano* was 38 miles outside the zone when it was torpedoed without warning, and many people have criticised the action. My own view is that it was justified. If you don't want your warships sunk, don't invade other people's territory – something, similarly, which happened without warning. It was a terrible tragedy for the guys who died and their families, of course, but that's war. Additionally, it also almost certainly shortened the conflict considerably, and saved hundreds of lives in the process: the Argentine navy was recalled to port after the sinking and played virtually no part in proceedings from that point on. An aggressive, committed enemy fleet would certainly have posed major problems to the Task Force, and might even have won Argentina the war.

At the time, none of this even entered my head amid all the cheering and celebrating going on around me as news broke. But I did realise that any doubts we had had about fighting a war had now gone.

Much worse was to come, and very shortly.

THIS IS WAR

I REMEMBER the evening of 4th May very well. We were not far from the Falklands now, all trying to relax and keep calm, some were writing letters home, or reading a book, that sort of thing when suddenly our Troop Commander came down the metal stairway and shouted for attention. I could tell by his expression he didn't have good news, I was right, he didn't. He didn't mince his words either. *HMS Sheffield* had been hit by an Exocet missile and had been destroyed. She had been on forward radar, scouting around seventy miles south east of Port Stanley about 50 km away, when a pair of French-made Super Etendard fighter-bombers from their mainland base of Rio Gallegos spotted her and *HMS Yarmouth* on radar. The planes headed closer and, at 20km, fired off a pair of AM39 Exocet missiles before peeling off for home.One of these missiles locked onto the Sheffield, and the other onto the Yarmouth.The Exocet missile, also French-made and helpfully supplied to the enemy by our garlic chomping friends across the Channel – it probably slipped their minds that we'd saved their backsides in two world wars – was a brilliant ship-killer; skimming six or eight feet above the waves at 700 miles per hour, they were terribly hard to detect and destroy or evade. The *Yarmouth* saw them coming and deployed chaff, strips of metal designed confuse the missile's radar. She was saved, but the *Sheffield* did not react in time and she was hit amidships. The explosion and subsequent fire killed 22 sailors and left 24 others severely injured.

When the Troop Commander stopped talking, there were a few moments of stony silence, just the humming of the ships engines, as the full impact of what we had just heard sank in.

There was no fucking doubt now; we were at war, good and proper.

After the shock, the initial response was one of fear, to be honest. Here we were, crammed into a flat-bottomed troop ship defended by obsolete Bofors anti-aircraft guns… we felt like the sitting ducks we were. What chance would we have of defending ourselves against a modern anti-ship weapon like Exocet, when a multi-million pound, state-of-the-art destroyer had just been taken out?

Then the fear turned to anger: the perfect antidote. Red, white and blue blood was pulsing through our veins, we were willing to defend our country's honour to the death. At that moment, as Maggie had said: 'Defeat? The possibility does not exist.'

The loss made me want to fight, to kill Argentineans. I hated them all. The *Sheffield* had been built in the shipyards close to my home town; I remembered how, while she had been under construction, a welder had been killed in a gas explosion. Folk locally had said afterwards that the ship would have no luck and now their predictions seemed to have come horribly true.

I wanted to play my own small part in settling the score: I'd teach the bastards to sink the shiny Sheff.

It didn't occur to me at the time, but the sinking of the *Belgrano* would have had the same effect on the Argentine forces, of course. Those Super Etendard pilots would have been seething after she went down and watching our frigate burn as they raced for home would have been the sweetest revenge for them. That's the dreadful irony of war; one set of families mourning behind closed doors, another set lining the streets cheering.

Back home, the politicians had been talking for weeks, trying to find a diplomatic solution, with various peace proposals being put forward by various people and rejected by one side or the other. The sinking meant all faint hopes of diplomacy had gone.

Not that we wanted diplomacy to work, now. In the beginning, if the whole crisis had been settled and we had turned around and gone home, I would have breathed a sigh of relief. Not now. Now I would have felt betrayed if I hadn't fought, even though I was scared absolutely shitless by the thought of it. The time for hot air was over; the outcome would be decided by bullet and bayonet. All of us were now totally committed to the task ahead.

On deck a day or two later, we noticed the Canberra sailing nearby. I could see the Paras running around on the ship, keeping fit, looking the business. It was a great sight: I realised that we weren't on our own and I think I also knew then that we would win the war. The thought of facing our Paras and Marines in battle… well, as the Duke of Wellington said, I didn't know what they were doing to the enemy, but by God they scared me. It wasn't much fun on the *Sir Geraint* and the fear of Exocet attack was still there, big-time, but things could definitely be worse: I could be a teenage Argie conscript, sitting in the shit and cold, waiting to be disembowelled by a British bayonet.

Like a lot of the guys in the last few days of the voyage, my mind was a bubbling pot of thoughts and emotions. My life was in danger now and, being human, I was scared. But I was proud to be there and more than anything I didn't want to let anyone down – my mates in the Battery, my family and friends, my home town, the whole of the country. In fact, I wanted – we all wanted – to show the whole world what happened when they messed with the Brits.

The strangest things go through your mind as you're sitting there, D-Day getting slightly closer every minute. I remember thinking to myself, I'm glad I got my end away. At least if I die, I won't die a cherry-boy. There must have been a few virgins amongst us, though this is definitely not the sort of thing that a soldier would admit (unless he was in a German brothel where, rumour had it, first-timers got a freebie. Sadly this never worked for me.). I thought about home, my family, Carole. I wondered what the lads I'd been at school with were doing now. I thought back over all the shit we'd all been through in juniors: the bed blocks, punishment parade, The Stream, days spent scraping the paint off a 'Brasso' tin until only the letters 'RA' were left, making your socks smile in your locker layout, keeping your toothpaste tube rectangular, polishing everything, polishing, polishing, polishing, all part of getting me here, getting me to war.

Early in May, the SAS and SBS made a daring raid on Pebble Island, a little outcrop north of West Falkland where the Argentineans had set up an airbase. In the style of their origins under David Stirling, they destroyed 11 Argentine aircraft in the attack. A ripple of applause went round the ship as the news of that one filtered out: nice one, lads that will give the Argies something to chew on. (The Royal Artillery played a part in this raid as a Captain Brown was the naval gun fire support forward observer from 148 Battery 29 Commando Regt RA. He called in the 4.5in guns of *HMS Glamorgan*, directing their shells, and why not? Let the senior service have a crack at the bastards as well.)

On the 10th of the month, all the top brass, including GBH, had a chinwag on board *HMS Fearless* to decide when and where we would go ashore. We didn't know it then – they tend not to advertise these things to the likes of us – but we only had another week at sea until we landed. The location had taken weeks of argument; luckily for us, there was a man on board who knew his stuff, a Major who had commanded NP8901, the Royal Marines garrison on the islands, prior to the Argentine invasion. He must have drawn the short straw for that job, given that until the first few swarthy South Americans walked ashore there hadn't been much in the way of entertainment on the island, but this was where the sheep shit was hitting the fan now and his input would have been invaluable.

The Argies had concentrated a lot of their troops around the capital, Port Stanley. They clearly thought that we would adopt similar tactics to those that the Yanks would have used – that is, to soften them up with bombing from the air for several days, then follow this up with shelling from the sea and, finally, launch a good, old-fashioned US Marines-style John Wayne, Audie Murphy kick-ass frontal-assault beach-landing.

Sorry, Diego, old bean, not the British way.

Instead, we would be landing at a place called San Carlos, fifty miles east.

* * * * *

Twelve hours to go until D Day – May 21, 1982.

After weeks of being at sea, we were almost ready. I suppose the longest night of all for any combat soldier is the eve of battle. All our equipment was checked and re-checked a dozen times, sometimes with shaky hands, as orders were given from London to *Fearless*, to our officers and then, finally, at the end of a very long chain, to us.

Our call sign was to be 32 Alpha: we were the third Battery in the Regt, the 2nd troop in the Battery, and first fire unit in the troop.

Bob, our sergeant, laid out the basic plan to us as we huddled round below deck.

We would be landing at San Carlos, on the west edge of East Falkland, around 50 miles away from Stanley, which was on the east coast of the island.

Phases One and Two of the landing would involve 40 Commando and 2 Para securing San Carlos settlement and 45 Commando and 3 Para taking Ajax Bay, just across

San Carlos Water, and Port San Carlos, which sat on another inlet around the headland to the north.

We were to be Phase Three, getting ashore and digging in with our missiles to provide air cover for the other troops and the ships in the bay from the Argentinean Skyhawks, Daggers and Mirages, plus their own Pucara close support aircraft, which would be coming at us in waves. Disgracefully, we would be limited to this role during daylight hours because we had not been supplied with a DN181 blind fire radar system. This would have given us the capacity to fire during hours of darkness, when the Mark One Eyeball is unfortunately obsolete. At the time, we just shrugged our shoulders and got on with it but, looking back, I feel extremely angry that soldiers can be sent to war, and put in harm's way, without the best equipment available to protect them and others. We'd used the bloody DN181 on exercise in Germany, when there was no danger and we weren't even firing live missiles, for goodness' sake. Now it mattered, we hadn't been given it. Someone's head – a senior officer, someone at the MoD, someone, somewhere – should have rolled. (Later, our position at San Carlos would be bombed one night by an enemy Canberra. The guy missed. If he hadn't, and he had killed our Rapier detachment, some pen-pusher, whether through penny-pinching or just incompetence, would have had our blood on his hands.)

We would be airlifted to our position, which had been selected for us by planners using computers designed to map out the best positions for all-round air defence coverage, after the second and third battalions Parachute Regt and 40, 42, and 45 Commando Royal Marines had cleared the ground.

Well, now we knew where we'd be going and what we'd be doing. It helped a bit, though I didn't like the fact that – unlike the first two phases – us crap hats would be going ashore in broad daylight. This didn't strike me as a very good idea at all.

I knew that I ought to get some rest, but apart from the odd catnap I couldn't sleep – there was too much adrenalin pumping around, too many wild thoughts. We were told that there would be a church service on board later that night and that we could attend of our own free will, religion being a personal matter, even in the Army. Though I was born a Catholic, I was not particularly religious, and didn't much bother with church normally. But it seemed prudent to change my habits, even if it was just a case of hedging my bets; there was a reasonable chance that I could be dead in a few hours, and I wanted to exit via the 'up' escalator if that happened. I polished my boots, brushed my beret, and set off for the Chapel, a small mess room. I was a few minutes early; there were only half a dozen people there, a few senior ranks and NCOs and a couple of buckshees like me. The Padre said a couple of prayers, made an observation or two, and the rest of the service was spent singing hymns – *For Those In Peril On The Sea* and *Jerusalem* struck me as being particularly relevant – and we finished off with a rousing chorus of *Land Of Hope And Glory*. On other visits to church, at Christmas and for weddings and the like, I tend to mumble along to the hymns, not really bothering to think about what the words mean. That night, I sang from the bottom of my heart, loud, not caring how tuneless I sounded. I have never enjoyed a church service more. It really made me feel protected, and as though I was on the good side in a crusade against evil.

God is watching over us. He will protect us. We're the good guys, aren't we?

I noticed on the way out that a lot more people had turned up after me. I saw a few faces that surprised me, and I think the feeling was mutual. It was almost as though the ship itself was sinking, and suddenly everyone was clutching a cross and a Bible and begging for forgiveness.

There was no humour, no piss-taking, as would generally be the norm, and we all filed off to re-check our equipment. Again. And then to re-read a book, page after page after page, without paying any attention to what the words said.

The ship was in the highest state of battle readiness now, darkened, all hatches sealed, everybody milling about their personal equipment in the eerie red emergency lighting. It reminded me a little of a Battery parade in a brothel, minus the whores.

I lay on my bunk, lots of weird and totally irrelevant thoughts bouncing around in my brain. I wished I was at home, taking Nickie my mongrel dog for a walk, coming through our door, Mam making the tea – sausage, mash and beans, all piled into a big mountain in the middle of my plate. I could see my dad coming in from work, unlike him not to go straight to the pub, and shouting at my poor Mam because there wasn't enough meat on his plate. My eyes closed, I could actually smell the chemicals on his clothes from the British Cellophane factory mixing in with the frying sausage.

Thoughts of Carole. I wished I was sat in her kitchen, door shut, the muffled sound of *Coronation Street* in the background as we have a quick snog. I wondered what she was doing… whether she'd be thinking of me, whether she'd have the slightest idea of what *I* was doing. I'd have given a lot to have been with her right then, to have someone say, 'It's all been a big mistake, Tony, and we're all going home.'

Then an NCO shouted, waking me from my daydream. 'Upstairs to collect your ammo!' he bawled. 'Single file! And keep the fucking noise down!'

Keep the fucking noise down? What about you?

I collected my stash: five magazines of 20 rounds 7.62mm rifle ammo, two L2 grenades, and four rounds for the Charlie G anti-tank weapon. The 84mm Karl Gustav, a medium-range anti-armour weapon, was a heavy bastard and so were its projectiles. I picked up my first field dressings, my morphine, and some ancillary equipment for the Rapier and a bone-dome (helmet).

We were told to double-check that we didn't have any personal items with us, letters, anything that could be useful to the enemy. I pictured the scene before the Argies kicked the living shite out me and put a round through my head.

The nice one, one of my letters from home in his hand, would be saying: 'Anthony, I see your mama is a proud Roman Catholic. I know it's not your fault you're in the Malvinas, the evil Thatcher sent you. She doesn't care about the poor soldiers she sends to war. Your mama and Jesus and I know that you being here is wrong, and so do you. You want to help us, don't you? Now, what Regiment are you in? Come, now. Tell us and you can have some corned beef and sleep.'

Me (assuming I was brave enough): 'Piss off.'

Biff, boff, lights out.

Letters from home? What am I on about? I didn't get a single letter from my parents in all the time I was away. At the time, I didn't give it a second thought, but in later years I've realised it's actually quite sad. Knowing someone is at home, who loves and cares about you, helps you to get through things. At least I didn't get any distractions to take my mind off the job, though.

Four hours to go.

I couldn't sit still, never mind sleep, so I decided to strip down my rifle and clean it again. It couldn't get any cleaner – it would have put a new one to shame – but it gave me something to concentrate on, something to do with my hands. That rifle loved me, because I loved it: it wouldn't jam on me while some sadistic Argie Special Forces bastard with a penchant for tearing men's gonads off with his bare hands ran towards me grinning from fat greasy ear to bloody ear.

All the time, singing to myself, under my breath: 'If I die in a combat zone, box me up and ship me home,' over and over again. Yes, I'd watched enough 'Nam films and read enough paperbacks to get me through this, piece of piss, no sweat.

Just to really make my day, one of the guys popped his head round the door.

'Have you heard the news, Mack?' he said, his face tight with tension. 'A Sea King has gone down in the sea. There were 18 SAS lads on board… they're all dead.'

That's a real morale booster, that is. The SAS are super-human, almost mythological beings that you never actually meet. SAS men can't die, they're indestructible. If they can die, I can *definitely* die. Shut up – they're not dead, it's all bollocks. They've probably swum ashore, probably *surfed* ashore on the busted-off rotor blades, and are, even now, tucked up nice and warm in some little farmhouse.

But the reality was that they *were* dead: exactly the same 'dead' as the sailors drowned, burned or blown apart on the *Sheffield* and the *Belgrano*. The chopper had gone down during a flight between two of our ships, killing a Signaller and an RAF man too. The ridiculous thing is, the crash was supposedly down to an albatross hitting the aircraft. A sodding albatross, it was almost comical if it wasn't so tragic. They're supposed to bring you good luck aren't they? As I sat there, their mates were probably already making jokes about it, the way soldiers do. They'd be gutted, angry, sad as you like, but they'd still be having the craic. It's a British thing, we're good at taking the piss out of ourselves, and squaddies are better than most. It's like a pressure release valve. I wondered how strong that valve would need to be other the coming weeks.

I finally managed to half-doze off, but it wasn't long before I was woken and ordered to the galley for breakfast – or 'The Last Supper', as we called it. The fear, stronger now, made me feel a little sick, but I stuffed as much bacon, sausage and egg down my throat as I could, as this was probably the last fresh rations I'd be eating for a while. Just as the last piece of bacon found its way into my belly, 40 Commando would be hitting San Carlos and 45 Commando getting stuck in at Ajax Bay.

God must have liked our singing in the chapel, because he'd laid on some thick fog and cloud and kept it nice and dark – though down there in the south, at that time of year, it doesn't get light till late on at the best of times.

One hour to go.

We edged towards East Falkland now, the ship vibrating gently as we made around 11 knots in the gentle swell.

I bet it's tense up on the bridge, I thought. *They'll be getting regular reports of air movements on the Argentine mainland from our intelligence-gathering teams, the SAS, the SBS and the James Bond-types. We might just be lucky and sneak up on the Argentineans; it doesn't look as though they anticipated us landing at San Carlos.*

Due to a small navigational error, we were about an hour behind schedule. But no air attacks, not a single one, on our amphibious force as yet.

Up top, the mist had started to lift and, as we bobbed around in a flat calm sea, beneath a beautiful, crystal-clear pre-dawn sky pitted with pin-sharp stars throwing faint light on the surrounding hills, an enemy Canberra bomber flew high overhead on a recon mission.

I imagine his eyes almost popped out of his head at the sight of us, far below.

He radioed Stanley and Buenos Aires with the bad news.

The radio chatter was soon flying back and forth, and was intercepted by the British SIGNET Signals Network. The spooks also heard excitable enemy reports of British troops landing in the south, at Goose Green. An

SAS team had staged a diversionary raid, calling in naval gunfire from our battleships while opening up with everything they have to make the enemy think that they are being attacked in battalion strength. To sow more confusion as to our actual landing place, *HMS Glamorgan* was operating in Berkeley Sound, shelling positions around Stanley, and further down Falkland Sound *HMS Ardent* was also letting rip; we could hear the gunfire in the distance.

* * * * *

It's a good job the landing wasn't heavily defended. I couldn't believe my eyes when I finally got up on deck.

It was broad daylight by that time and, sitting there in the still waters, in just about the calmest, clearest conditions you could imagine, were dozens of our ships. They were all around us, helicopters buzzing overhead like swarms of bees. It was a lovely day for a war.

I thought to myself, *This is unreal; it's just like a big exercise. Where's the enemy? And can we get off this bloody ship before they arrive, please?*

In my mind, I had conjured up visions of an invasion like the Normandy beach landings of World War II, with hundreds of warships shelling the coast, thousands of men surging ashore in landing craft, enormous noise and activity, dug-in enemy hosing our boys down with machine guns as they struggled onto the sand or died in the water. I could hear sporadic firing in the distance, and the odd muffled explosion, but overall it was very quiet. I started to relax a little: things rarely turn out how you imagine them and if this was war it wasn't too bad after all.

I remember breathing in the fresh salty air. The odd sea bird flying about… if you could shut out the noise of the aero engines and the distant skirmishing, it was just like being on board a pleasure boat on Lake Windermere back home.

One big difference – you don't get attacked from the air on Lake Windermere, unless you count seagulls crapping in your chips.

Suddenly, I heard the noise of close-up machine gun fire and spun around, crouching down instinctively as I did so. A Pucara 339 twin-propeller-driven fighter flown by Lt Crippa roared overhead, the sun glinting off its fuselage as it fired salvoes of rockets at *HMS Argonaut*, just missing, and banking to have a crack at the large, white bulk of the *Canberra*. Luckily, he missed again – probably shocked at the size of the armada which had appeared in front of him as he'd flown over the hill. He didn't have long to reflect on his misses, either. He was engaged by Royal Marine Ricky Strange of Air Defence troop, firing his Blowpipe missile which were lashed to the Canberra's rails and lots of GPMG fire but Lt Crippa incredibly made it back to base. Ricky strange went on to successful destroy a Aermacchi MB339 at Goose Green.

It seemed surreal, standing there with my mates watching missiles and cannon fire streaking through the sky, and huge geysers erupting around the ships. It was as though it was all just a laid-on aerobatic display or something from a film set. Somewhere in the back of my brain, the fight or flight instinct was trying to warn me that I was in danger but, like a moth to the flame, I kept on watching.

I saw brave pilot shot down, a martyr of the Argentine brought to earth by a 5.5in shell fired from one of our frigates. There wasn't much time to enjoy the moment though; I was just relieved we were OK. We were to be ferried ashore with our equipment by helicopter – ahead of the 29 Commando gunners, since Rapier had more chance of hitting an attacking jet than a 105mm light gun shell – and our lift-off times were chalked on a blackboard.

Our detachment was one of the first to go, which suited me down to the ground. In a life-threatening situation you become selfish; we all felt very exposed on the ship and everyone was keen to get ashore before more Argie planes came our way. It wasn't naked fear, though. I was frightened, of course, but there was a lot of excitement and anticipation mixed in, too: it was similar to the feeling as you board a roller coaster or when doing a parachute jump – you're scared, but you're looking forward to it at the same time. I watched the first couple of choppers take the detachments in front of us and shuffled along to wait my turn. It was a cold day, but I was sweating like a pig. My heart was beating fast and I could hear the blood surging in my ears and I constantly scanned the horizon for enemy aircraft. Eventually, our Sea King helicopter chopper landed on the Heli-deck with a slight bounce and the doorman urgently signalled us forward. Grabbing my rifle and heavy equipment, I followed Bob and the others and, crouched awkwardly under the weight of my webbing and its contents, jogged into the aircraft. The wop, wop, wop of the rotors was deafening – the pilot had kept it at full throttle for a quick take-off – and we communicated only by hand-signals once on board. The heat from the engines blasted my face, along with the familiar smell of all choppers – aviation fuel and rubber. Again, it felt strangely like an exercise, except that the door gunner was crouched over a loaded GPMG hooked up to a belt of 7.62mm link ammo, and he looked very ready to fire it.

Now all aboard, we powered into the air then banked to the left, dropping down and heading for land, just skimming the waves, the g-force leaving my body feeling like a heavy weight had been pressed on my head. It's a cliché but all my senses were going into overdrive. We were probably airborne for a couple of minutes at most, but it felt a good deal longer than that. My biggest fear was of being hit by a missile. I kept thinking of ditching into the sea below. *I'm bound to drown*, I thought. In combat there was no room for life jackets and I wasn't much of a swimmer. With the huge weight of ammo and equipment I would surely plummet into the icy depths, like a house brick into a pond. *I'll settle for dying on the ground like soldiers are supposed to.* The idea of being eaten by fish was disgusting, more powerful than the fear of death itself. To take my mind off it, I remember humming Wagner's *Ride of the Valkyries*, played from speakers slung underneath Colonel Kilgore's attack helicopter in the movie *Apocalypse Now*. Then suddenly there was green beneath us and the chopper was flaring as the pilot brought her down on a flat section of ground overlooking the bay. I didn't know what to expect – probably a hail of machine gun fire. I knew our special forces had been in action, along with some of the Paras and Marines, but I still expected to be set down in a hot LZ, as they say in the movies. Well, I was just a nineteen-year-old kid, and this was my first war.

We landed and we sat there for a second, not quite sure how to react. Then we all piled out and took up a position of all-round defence, rifles at the ready, in case of surprise attack.

Right, let's go you bastards, I'm thinking, as I lie there in a fire position, finger on the trigger, waiting for the inevitable attack.

The only resistance we met was from our BQMS staff, who sauntered over, all nonchalant and grinning.

'All right lads,' said one of them. 'What took you so long? Fancy a brew?'

I was a bit shocked but very relieved as I stared in disbelief at them, casually brewing up and having a fag and a laugh, like this was a Sunday afternoon picnic.

Perhaps it *was* just an exercise after all?

We passed on the brew and set about getting the system operational. It seemed to take forever as we had to wait for the helicopters to bring everything over. It took several loads per detachment, a lot of kit all slung under one of the Task Force's Sea King workhorses. After we were dropped off to secure our position, we had to wait for the launcher, then the one tonne DSV (Detachment Supply Vehicle) that had the optical tracker and radio in the back, then extra Rapier missiles under slung in cargo nets, then food and extra small arms ammunition. All around, the air was frantically buzzing with choppers like busy worker bees, dropping off men and supplies.

We worked as quickly as possible to get the Rapier into action, all the time thinking about our lack of cover and nervously eyeing the skies. In our NATO role, we were used to being deployed on, say, the edge of a wood, with a lot of overhanging foliage under which to hide. Here, it was like the hills around my Cumbrian home town, though unlike back home there was not a tree in sight; in fact, there was nothing for miles and miles but soggy, peaty grass and scrub. We were very exposed, although we had prepared for this as best we could, bringing our own camouflage netting and poles from England. These were enough to conceal us from a casual observer but we knew that if the enemy decided specifically to target Rapier sites we were in trouble. All we could do was hope and pray they didn't, and dig in to give ourselves the best chance possible if they did. Digging in is bread and butter work to a soldier; we chopped away at the black earth with our spades, hollowing out trenches for ourselves and for the equipment, and burying the cables to protect them in the event of attack. The ground was very wet, though, and as soon as you dug out a chunk of the earth the hole would start to fill up with filthy, foul-smelling water. This led to a lot of our infantry going down with 'Trench Foot', a condition more readily associated with the First World War. This is an infection of the feet caused by standing for hours on end in cold, wet and unsanitary conditions. If untreated, it can turn gangrenous and result in amputation. They solved the problem back in WWI by ordering soldiers to change their socks at least twice a day and forcing them to smear grease made from whale oil on their feet. Luckily, 32 Alpha never got to the point of needing whale oil.

We were still a long way off being operational when the first air attack warnings came, with the words 'Air Raid Warning Red' sounding over on the radio to indicate that bogeys (enemies) were heading our way.

Oh shit, this is for real…people are trying to kill us! Call the police!

Everybody scrambled into life, running here and there; trying frantically to get into position to engage the enemy if he appeared. We all had specific jobs to do, but we always seemed to find things were not running according to the drill book; everyone was trying to do everything single-handed in a sort of organised panic. It was futile and we were hardly ready when they showed up some way down the coast. The first thing I heard was the immense noise of all our guns blazing, troops on the ground firing everything into the air, the ships in the sound firing missiles, anti-aircraft guns firing on the landing craft, one huge great November 5.

Then came that unmistakable noise of jet engines screeching all around and the enormous thunderclaps of the ships anti-aircraft guns, the sound echoing along the valleys – a noise that even today makes the hairs on the back of my neck stand on end and leaves me with an overwhelming urge to find the source of the noise, eyeball it and get down low.

Then, as quickly as they'd arrived, they were gone. One thing in our favour was that most of the Argentinean aircraft were operating at the limit of their fuel – they only had time for a few minutes over their targets before they had to turn tail and scoot home. The firing died down and everyone continued digging in. Fifteen minutes later, the bastards were back – including my friend in the A4 – in a pattern which was to continue for most of the day. Lads were ducking down or trying to engage the enemy with their personal weapons. As I've said, it seems a little futile firing a rifle at a fast jet, but every little helps and when added to the rest of the lead flying about it must have been difficult for the pilots to keep their sites lined up on our frigates, which were obviously their main target. And in fact, there were reports throughout the war of enemy planes being brought down by small arms fire. Range wasn't a problem: they were so low to the ground you could clearly see the pilots and read the markings on the fuselage. The trick was to aim ahead of where they were, so that they would fly into your bullets.

Earlier that day, some British blood had been spilled. The night before, on the eve of D Day, a small reconnaissance unit of SBS from *HMS Brilliant* had gone ashore to double-check that San Carlos was still undefended, as was thought to be the case. They were shocked to hear Spanish voices in the dark, and hastily paddled back in their canoes to report their findings. A larger force of SBS was dispatched, with orders to capture the enemy if possible. The Argies weren't too keen on being taken prisoner – we later heard they had been told by their superiors that British troops were cannibals and would eat them alive, which was effective propaganda, if nothing else. After a brief firefight, they legged it into the hills. Then, on the morning of D Day itself, the Paras found evidence that a further, larger group of Argies had scarpered just in time, leaving their warm breakfasts behind.

This meant a group of armed enemy soldiers, albeit in retreat, were in the area. Unfortunately, this information didn't get passed on to the helicopter pilots who were about to start lifting us ashore. One of our Sea Kings, carrying some missiles and heading for a Rapier site with a Royal Marine Gazelle escort, flew straight above the enemy troops from San Carlos. They opened up on both choppers with heavy machine gun fire. The Sea King managed to escape, but the Gazelle took the full brunt of the fire but the pilot managed to turn away from the enemy and ditch in the sea.

In a sickening moment, the defenceless crew were then machine-gunned in the water; one, Sgt Andy Evans, was dragged from the water by locals but sadly died from his injuries in his colleague's arms.

A quarter of an hour later, a second Gazelle fell victim in the same way, raked by machine gun fire from below and crashing to the ground in flames. Rescuers managed to drag the bodies from the wreckage, but they were already dead with machine gun rounds in their chests. That first incident, by the way, with unarmed aircrew being fired on in the water, was to set the tone for the rest of the war: hatred and mistrust were rife. But then war is a dirty, nasty business at the best of times.

So, three dead already. I suppose, compared to other operations, the statisticians would say that three killed during the landings was very good. But they were still tragic incidents.

We settled into our wartime routine, a routine that wouldn't change until the end of the conflict. Rapier consists of a launcher, which is shaped a bit like a large dustbin with four missile tubes attached, an optical tracker, where the operator sits to control and fire the missiles, and a generator to provide electrical power. Throughout all the daylight hours, one man would sit in the seat of the tracker in 'stags' of four hours at a time. Standing alongside him would be another soldier (usually an NCO) for tactical control purposes; he would control the engagement of enemy aircraft and give the order 'Engage', to fire the missile. The rest of the detachment would be on stag watching for any approach by enemy ground forces, or unloading the next missiles to be fired, or preparing a meal and the continuous brews – a Godsend, believe me, when you've been sat in the same position for hours, the wind gusting and the cold and rain making your body numb. The Jerry can supplying the generator had to be regularly checked for petrol, the radio had to be manned and those not needed were allowed to rest in between being rotated to and from the tracker seat.

The generator, by the way, is about the size of a tumble drier and very loud – I was told it had the same engine as the old Hillman Imp – and that led to some amusing incidents on exercise. We would be moving into a tactical position with lots of other Regiments nearby, all trying to be inconspicuous and quiet, cam-creamed-up, netting everywhere, no speaking and everyone communicating with hand signals. Then, out of the blue would come the ungodly screaming of the good old Rapier generator. It was a horrible noise and used to piss off a lot of other units who were ignorant of how Rapier worked; they didn't realise that that noise meant you had air defence cover.

Well, sometimes you had.

As I mentioned earlier, Rapier was a very temperamental weapons system and a thousand and one things could go wrong with it. We were concerned about the battering it had taken on the voyage over, and also about the heavy handling of the helicopter crews, who naturally wanted to get rid of any cargo they were carrying and get airborne again ASAP. They didn't seem to know it needed treating with kid gloves and didn't bounce very well.

One thing we noticed straight away was a serious issue with our radar and IFF system.

Rapier, in theory, works by picking up a target on the radar, which is switched on to detect any approaching threat. The alarm tone sounds in the operator's helmet as the missiles and tracker head automatically swivel to line up in the direction of the potentially hostile aircraft. As the

IFF interrogation takes place, the operator responds by acquiring the aircraft in a wide field of view with the optical sights, which work to a distance of about 11.5k. As the plane gets closer, he switches to a narrow field and tries to keep it in the cross-hairs of the optics. Inside the sight are four lights, each with different meanings. The top right light means 'Out Of Cover' – the aircraft is outside the system's range. The top left light means that the operator has to 'Wait' – the target is about to come into range. The bottom right light means the system doesn't know whether it's in range or not – not all that helpful, to be honest. The light you want to see illuminated is the bottom left hand one, which means 'In Cover'. Then you know that the target is within Rapier's 6.5k range and you can kill it.

If the IFF has identified it as enemy, the operator – once given the order by an NCO – can press the fire button to engage it. Using a joystick and keeping the cross-hairs on the target, a bit like a primitive arcade game by today's standards, then he steers the missile towards the plane hopefully with a hit at the end. It was possible for an operator accidentally to 'track' his own missile when it entered his field of view, mistaking it for the target. This did actually happen during the war. And, no, it wasn't me. Assuming you do everything right, you'll hit the target, which you do need to do: unlike modern weapons, Rapier didn't have proximity fuses so you actually had to hit whatever you were aiming at to stand any chance of destroying it (so it's actually a 'hittile', not a missile).

All fine, in theory. However, because of a variety of faults, our Rapier kept alarming on friendly helicopters. The potential dangers are obvious; a moment's loss of concentration, a slip of the thumb, and a Gazelle is destroyed and your own men killed. Because of this, we decided we had no alternative but to switch the radar and the IFF system off and go purely optical. This meant our range was reduced – we needed to be able to see a target in order to engage it. We were still capable of locating, hitting and destroying the enemy. But against fast jets, flying low and arriving with little warning, it cut our reaction time down to a matter of seconds. And it was only the first problem to dog our equipment. Later, other elements of our Rapier would malfunction; when that happened, the consequences would be serious and tragic.

OUR BOYS ARE DYING

Once on the ground, we soon lost track of what day it was. If it was night time, we were lying shivering in our trenches, cuddling our rifles, eyes and ears straining for the arrival of Argentine Special Forces, as we knew that they would be looking for the Rapier crews. If it was day time, we were rotating through the firing seat of the Rapier, loading missiles or making brews and personal admin.

We had heavy air attacks for a fair while, until substantial Argentine losses meant they eventually had to pull back and cut down their operations – the beginning of the end for them in what was a war which would, essentially, be decided by air superiority. In the early days in San Carlos, though, there was no hint of that; the Argies were really trying to hammer the ships in the sound, which was not surprising, and they had some success because there were so many targets for them to choose from.

Along with other Rapier teams – and anti-aircraft crew on the ships themselves, Harriers and even the infantry – we were in action almost constantly from D Day onwards, desperately trying to bring down enemy jets or at least put them off their aim. More often than not, the furious hail of lead and high explosive worked. But there were some brave lads at the controls of those aircraft, flying like they drove their Ferraris back home in Buenos Aires, and sometimes they managed to get through.

We had lost the *Sheffield* two or three weeks earlier and *HMS Glasgow* had been hit on May 12. On May 21, *Antrim*, *Broadsword*, *Argonaut* and *Brilliant* were also hit. The damage to *Broadsword* and *Brilliant* was caused by cannon strafing, and was fairly light, but *Antrim* and *Argonaut* (like *Glasgow*) had very lucky escapes. Each was hit by bombs which failed to explode; if they had detonated, the ships would almost certainly have been sunk. The consequent loss of life would have been dreadful enough but the loss of the ships might well have cost us the war. The number of these UXBs was almost freakish and was probably caused by the combination of the terrain and our air defences. The enemy pilots had to swoop in fast and launch their bombs from a low altitude at the very last moment. Their fuses needed time to time in the air to arm themselves and they often didn't get it so they simply never exploded.

HMS Ardent wasn't so lucky, however. She was attacked the same day by eight Daggers in Grantham Sound, the next inlet along from San Carlos, and hit with cannon fire and nine 500lb bombs, three of which did go off. She survived and was limping for cover when she was attacked and hit again. Those bombs exploded, too, and she was lost, finally sinking the following day. There were 199 men on board when the first attack happened, and their average age was just 23; 22 sailors were killed and 30 injured. It was terrible news, and it sent shock-waves through the lads; as a Rapier crew, the pressure we felt to strike back at the enemy, to put our own stamp on the course of the war, was enormous. Our boys were dying out there, and every plane that got past us was like a knife in our own ribs.

Despite the almost constant threat, no-one can maintain perfect concentration for days on end. It would be relatively calm for half an hour or so. I would sit in the seat on my stag and I'd practice by tracking our helicopters, which were still working feverishly, ferrying stores and ammo ashore, stopping every now and descending to hover near the ground as enemy aircraft zoomed into view for another attack. Or I'd watch long columns of our infantry disappearing in their hundreds into the hills like lines of ants. I remember wondering what they were going to come up against, and realising how much more frightened I'd be if I was one of them. Yes, we were at risk, and serious risk, but the ultimate in combat must be fighting to the death with another man, hand-to-hand, bayonet, boots, teeth, and entrenching tool, anything to stay alive and kill the other guy. Of course, we were infantry-trained ourselves: if our Rapier was destroyed, we would be up there alongside them.

There were moments when the possibility of proper fighting came closer. I recall one early morning – I must have been on my four hours off in my doss bag, and the Antarctic sun was just emerging over the horizon when Bob shook me awake. 'Mack,' he whispered, urgently. 'Get your kit on, weapon and get outside now.'

I grabbed my webbing and rifle and joined him and the rest of a slightly dishevelled-looking 32 Alpha. Bob was talking to a Royal Marine Captain who was asking how many men we were.

'Seven,' said Bob, as I rubbed my eyes and tried not to yawn.

'Right,' said the Captain. 'We've received intelligence that the enemy is planning to make a counter attack, a beach landing with assault craft, down there this morning.' He pointed at the nearest bit of coast, a few hundred yards away. 'We're short of men so until reinforcements get here we're going to need you guys to assist.'

The cobwebs of sleep were blown from my head the moment he said this, to be replaced by mental images of hand-to-hand combat with desperate Latino squaddies. It was a scary thought, but we were soldiers: we grabbed every weapon, round and grenade we could find, stuffing our pockets with extra 7.62mm till we all looked like Michelin men, and watched the Royal Marine stride away. At least he looked like he knew what he was doing.

Trenches were dug a little deeper, our rifles and our LMG were cleaned and oiled again and the radio was manned constantly as we anxiously scanned the sea, looking for any sign of the enemy in the grey morning light.

'You know what, Bob?' I said. 'If they do show up we ought to use the Rapier on them.'

He nodded. After all, four high explosive missiles hitting your boat at Mach 2 is going to put anyone off. But we waited and waited and they never came, and by mid-morning we stood down and went into our normal anti-aircraft search drills. Who knows how we would have reacted under fire? I don't think we would have disgraced the Royal Artillery or ourselves but part of me was glad we didn't get the chance to find out, but at the end of the day we were all soldiers first.

* * * * *

I am once again sitting in the tracker seat, scanning the area and wondering if I will ever see England again, when Bob brings me back to the reality of the here-and-now: 'Air Raid Warning Red, nine bogeys from the west, sixty miles, closing fast,' he shouts.

Here we go again.

The rest of the unit race to put their tin lids on and get into the cover of our water filled muddy trenches.

I'm thinking: *Shit, why am I always in the bastard seat when there's an air raid?*

I can't go anywhere, though: I have to stay put and see what happens.

I am now inside my own world. Nobody else exists except me, my rapidly-beating heart and the enemy aircraft screaming towards us. My eardrums are assaulted by a crescendo of noise as the guns on the ships in the bay below open up… every man, Jack, and his dog letting loose with everything from GPMGs to 9mm pistols. The high-pitched screech of low-flying jets reverberates all around me.

My eyes are pressed firmly into the optics, Bob is screaming 'targets' as he slews the optical tracker head in the direction of the attacking jets.

'Target tracking,' I shout.

Which one? It's strange, like in slow motion.

There's Sky Hawks and Mirages or Daggers, the Sky Hawks bright, naval white and the Mirages and Daggers with big, delta wings which are hard to see as they tip upwards, the sun glinting from the air-frames, camouflaging them against the landscape. I steady my thumb and forefinger on the joystick and the lamp in the bottom left hand corner of the optical sight illuminates.

'In cover!'

I press the fire button.

BANG! The noise of my missile leaving the beam is louder still than the cacophony around me. It streaks into the air but drops uselessly into the sea a few seconds later.

'A fucking rogue!..... Bastard!'

I search frantically for targets, tiny noisy things, fast-moving and incredibly hard to pick up and stay with, and find one. `In cover`. I fire again. Like the first one, this missile veers wildly off target too.

  Not Good.

I press the fire button yet again.

BANG! 'Missile in flight.'

Thank fuck this one has gathered ok, I thought

Keeping the cross-hairs on the centre of the target Skyhawk.

I must ignore my own missile flare appearing in my optics.

Bob's screaming, 'Target! Target!'

My missile appears in my sight – careful, remember that's you, not him. It has nearly reached its maximum Speed of Mach 2. As I watch with great relief as, my missile hits the A4 and detonates inside the aircraft, just below the cockpit... **BANG!** Large ball of flame, direct hit, smouldering burning parts of the jet disintegrate and fall down and splash into the sea below. I was like a well-oiled machine now, going through my drills, that was one Sky Hawk gone, no longer a threat to the Task-force, and it all happened in a matter of seconds, life and death in the blink of an eye.

Did the pilot get out? I didn't see, but at that understandably selfish moment I didn't care either, I was just another component in the missile system.

The sea below is being peppered with rockets and bombs, machine gun tracer is filling the sky, and the noise was unbelievable, nothing in training can prepare you for this moment, but the drills work, Rapier can be a lethal killer.

'End of engagement, search cancel... fresh target tracking... in cover... firing.'

Nothing happens. What's happening? I press again, and get the same result. Bob looks at me and I look at him.

'Shit! I've run out of missiles!' This could only happen in the mayhem of battle.

We both sprint down to the launcher to reload. I open a container, it hisses as the air is let in and a sweet smell, like warm honey, enters my nostrils. It's usually a careful two-man lift in peacetime – they're big things, Rapier missiles, 7ft 4in long and they weigh close to 50 kilos – and you should take your time, too, don't trap your fingers on the beams as happened to one Gunner who lost a finger. With the adrenalin flowing, we pick up a missile and slot them on as if they were made of balsa wood, we don't even notice the weight. We connect the firing lines which will initiate the launch and then leg it back to the tracker. I suppose it's a bit like when someone lifts up the weight of a car to free someone trapped underneath, they find strength from somewhere.

I can see other missiles being fired from our ships like camera flashes, and other T Battery Rapier detachments firing from the hillsides, it's a full on battle of San Carlos now.

A second wave of enemy, A4s and Mirages, scream overhead and attack the multiple naval targets in the sound, *My God look how many there are*, I think privately to myself.

HMS Fearless is nearly hit by several thousand-pound bombs.

'Target tracking… in cover… firing.'

Another missile streaks off the beam, before spinning out of control and exploding into the ground.

'Fuck! Search cancel… tracking… in cover… firing.'

This one's a good missile.

I have my sights lined up on the delta winged Mirage.

My finger and thumb are gently nudging the joystick, trying to keep the cross hairs in the centre of the fuselage.

He swoops in and drops his bombs, then rolls to the left, showing me his belly, sticks it into top gear and puts his foot down on the after-burners, heading for the open sea and home, while trying to dodge the wall of British tracer rounds all around him.

'Come on you bastard.'

I can see the flare of my missile coming into focus in my field of view.

Bob yells: 'The bastard's getting away.'

But I can see the projectile homing in on his exhaust, just a few more seconds please.

'Hit!'

'Yes!'

The missile was nearly at the last second of its life when it strikes the rear of the jet. I see the Mirage's tail fin explode and separate before the aircraft spins out of control corkscrewing spewing smoke, downwards and out of my view behind the hills, another bogey neutralised.

One of our other crews further along the valley, 31 Delta, watches it plummet into the ocean and a platoon of Royal Marines near us cheer and throw their green berets in the air in celebration confirmation of my kill, their GPMG barrels still smoking and glowing hot from all the lead they fired in to the sky.

Then, very quickly, the noise dies down and something approaching normality returns. The attack is over, and the anti-aircraft fire peters out to just a few pops. There's always some optimistic bastard who fires his last

SMG round at an aircraft's dispersing vapour trails. This is the norm in 'Bomb Alley'

(After the war, the number of kills officially credited to Rapier will be argued over for years and never finally resolved: the claims and counterclaims as to the numbers of enemy aircraft destroyed by the system vary from as high as 20 to as low as two. We stand by our kills, that's for sure: Bob communicated them to the Battery Headquarters and the rest of the lads, plus those Royal Marines, were in no doubt: we'd just destroyed two Argie planes – the only ones I would personally shoot down in the conflict.) But 32 Alpha wasn't finished just yet.

I hope the pilots got out alive – I don't want to have killed anyone – but I don't know whether they did, the Skyhawk pilot must have been killed. That wasn't going through my head at the time. I didn't even have time to think about the events that had just occurred, even to be pleased about hitting targets. It was a huge part of my young life but a very small part of the war going on around me. Just another day at the office; I continued with my drill of looking for more aircraft.

There was no back-slapping or celebrations from the other lads, either. I was tapped on the shoulder, turned around and there was Mickey Quinn, holding a large mug of steaming hot tea in his hand.

'Oh cheers, Quinny,' I said, holding out my hand.

'Fuck off, it's not for you,' he said, pulling it away and looking daggers at me. 'I'm on stag now. Go and make your own bastard.'

Yes, 32 Alpha was a generous detachment and we just got on with it.

Quinny was a good lad, a great laugh on a night out and a good boxer, a junior Army champion. He'd been like a bear with a sore arse the last day or so, and we noticed the side of his mouth had swollen up. It turned out he had an abscess under a rotten tooth. It doesn't seem that serious when gauged against people being shot down and blown up all around, but he couldn't do his job properly and he was hacking Bob and the rest of us off with his whinging.

What I am going to tell you now is the sort of thing you hear in the local TA bar, when someone starts putting more beer than lemonade in their pint pot. But I was that man; I did witness a Royal Army Medical Corps operation.

A medic came up to our position and asked where the casualty was. We told him he was the lad in the trench with the LMG and the gobstopper in his mouth, the lad who was probably going to advise him to go forth and multiply. The medic knew how to break the ice; I watched him wander over and produce a large bottle of whiskey. Quinny smiled for the first time in several days and proceeded to get stuck into it.

Suddenly, the whole of 32 Alpha had developed a toothache, with chants of 'I don't believe you, Quinny, stuck in the armpit of the universe and you get the finest malt whiskey, hand-delivered' echoing around our part of the Falklands.

His ecstasy soon turned to agony, though, as, with the aid of an Army right-angled torch and a pair of rusty pliers, the medic ripped the offending tooth straight out of Quinny's gob. It's rumoured that the same medic later got a job-working freelance for Saddam Hussein's military intelligence.

It wasn't all work in the Malvinas. Some days the sky would be clear and this pale yellow thing would appear up there. I remember seeing a similar one in

England from time to time, but the one down there must have been bust because it didn't give off any heat.

You'd get days which were perfect for enemy air activity, when the adrenalin would be pumping from first light until last, and nothing happened.

Let's get the football out.

Oh, we didn't bring one.

Never mind, I've got an idea, where's Ricky?

Poor old Ricky. He was the youngest NIG and more to the point, the smallest and the quietest in 32 Alpha. So Benny, Scouse and I chased our little mascot around, caught him, stripped him naked and staked him to the ground with tent pegs and bungees. We all thought this was highly amusing. Benny ran off, sniggering, and returned with a can of condensed milk which he proceeded to squirt all over Ricky's bollocks.

'Look everyone, Ricky's had a wet dream!'

I grant you, it's not the height of sophistication, humour-wise, but it tickled Benny. Well, it takes all sorts, I suppose.

By this time, Ricky was getting a lot of goose pimples and was begging to be released.

'In a minute matey,' I said. 'Just one last test of your nerves.'

I jumped in the one tonne Land Rover and drove it up to Ricky's head, just nudging him with the tyre. Things were getting a bit out of hand; give a squaddie an inch and he'll take the M6. Bob would have gone ape shit if he'd known what we were up to, but I think he was getting some shut-eye. Rank has its privileges. Instead, we were caught red-handed by the Troop Commander Lt Waddle, known as 'The Milky Bar Kid' for obvious reasons.

We got the usual Officer-type bollocking: what if we were bumped by the enemy? and that sort of thing, but I think he realised we were just letting off a bit of steam. I detected a slight smile on his lily-white face, hint of cam-cream on his brow, as he daintily tiptoed back down hill to the Milky Bar ranch. A fine officer I would have the privilege of meeting again on the same Islands twenty five years later.

That was a rare bit of levity, though. Due to the harsh weather conditions, most of our energy was used up in keeping warm and staying alive. We didn't know whether this conflict would go on for weeks, months or years. It certainly looked as though the Government was expecting it to take some time, as it was announced that on 1st June the men of the 5th Infantry Brigade were due to arrive to reinforce us. The good thing was the Gurkhas were part of this force: the general consensus was that once they started lopping heads off with their kukris the Argies were bound to jack.

WATCHING MEN BURN

After weeks aboard the *RFA Sir Geraint* and days dug in to the side of this miserable hill with precious little sleep and absolutely no Persil Automatic (other brands are available), we were beginning to look like something from the Dirty Dozen. We didn't have time for all the parade ground bullshit, and washing every day as you do when on exercise had gone by the by due to more pressing matters like trying to shoot down enemy aircraft. Faced with a choice of using our meagre water supply for washing the cam-cream off our faces, so we can put more cam-cream back on, or using it to make a nice hot cup of tea, well, I'll use it for tea, thanks. How come Charles Bronson always had a face full of stubble *and* a hot brew in the movies?

Most of the time it was blowing a gale, with sleet and hail that lashed horizontally into you and stung any exposed flesh. Most days, wind chill meant it was well below zero: just the usual Falklands climate during the balmy summer of 1982.

One morning, I noticed some bodies in all-round defence near our position. It was obvious they were Brits from their huge great Bergen rucksacks – which was a good job, given the fact that I hadn't spotted them arrive – and eventually it dawned on me that the Gurkhas had arrived. You could just see their little legs sticking out at the bottom and I remember thinking, *Thank God I'm just a crap hat and I don't have to lug all that shit around.* They sat there for hours, just getting wetter and colder. Being just a buckshee squaddie, I put myself in their position and realised I'd be ticking like fuck by now, especially if I was from the hot climate of Nepal. As a static Rapier position, we had reasonable cooking facilities – it wasn't exactly the Hilton, but we could rustle up a couple of wets. I mentioned this and my idea found its way along the chain of command – from me to Benny, from Benny to Taff, Taff to Bob and Bob to the Milky Bar Kid. Our offer of hospitality was approved and eagerly accepted by the Nepalese lads, and we quickly got the kettle on for them. Even though they were shivering in their boots they consider it an honour to be invited to our little bit of England – and what a jolly decent chap our TC was, having an idea like that! It was the first time that I'd seen a Ghurkha up close and they were very different to how I'd imagined them: they were great little guys, very humble, quiet and happy with their lot, despite the conditions. As an added bonus, they ended up stopping the night when their choppers were re-routed to another task. A couple of them kipped in our latrine trench and they didn't even moan about that, though it can't have been the greatest night of their lives. Having these boys sitting nearby on stag all night gave us the safest and most relaxed few hours of the whole operation by a considerable distance. We shook hands with them the next day and I watched as these walking Bergens disappeared into the hills, keen to get some South American blood on their kukris. It made you shudder to think; glad they were on our side.

The air raids continued, but the gaps between them became longer as the enemy lost a lot of aircraft on each sortie – depending which reports you believe, and they're confused because the Argentineans have never properly confirmed them – up to fifteen aircraft went down a day. 32 Alpha didn't play any more part in those kills at San Carlos, though. To add to our malfunctioning radar/IFF system, we now had a faulty tracker head. The tracker head's job was to be the eyes of the missile. Because of the IFF fault, Bob would physically spin it in the direction of the attacking aircraft as I picked it up in the bi-ocular sight. Sometimes it worked, and sometimes it didn't, and if it didn't we were U/S. it was clear that we needed REME assistance to get it fixed. While we did our best, I'm sure with our kit blob-on we would have had more successes.

The main ordnance used by the enemy aircraft was high explosive bombs, rockets and cannon-fire, but on the odd raid they used retard bombs, floating killer that descend slowly, swaying underneath parachutes. That really freaked me out: these things just seemed to hanging there forever, directly above my head, just taking the piss. Nasty bit of kit, I'd rather not see the fucker before it turned me into compost, thanks. Luckily, none of these hit our position though some landed too close for comfort and shook the ground around our trenches and one did explode on a trench nearby killing a sapper called Ghandi.

We were in almost as much danger from our own side, to tell the truth. One day a stray shells fired by our Gunner buddies from 4 Field Regt RA (Paras) landed very near to us. That would have been a nice way to go, a blue-on-blue incident with some moron from Colchester or Cornwall pulling the plug on you.

I had a chance to slot a Sergeant Major, and I was to live to regret not continuing with the second pressure on my trigger. In wartime, as on exercise, you are given a daily password, with a challenge and a response. For instance, the challenge might be 'Bravo Oscar' and the response 'Charlie Sierra'. The only difference is that is not particularly good for your health to forget the bastard password in wartime. Unless you have a death wish or you're a REMF (Rear-Echelon Mother-Fucker) who'd rather be beasting recruits at Woolwich.

I was on stag. It was just getting dark when I heard movements to my rear. I spun around in the direction of the noise and saw a shadowy figure coming towards me. My throat contracted and my mouth dried instantly, so I could hardly get the words out.

'Halt! Bravo Oscar!'

'It's me, Geordie.'

Wrong answer.

'Bravo Oscar!'

Cock weapon.

'It's me! Geordie! The TSM!'

This is in a mildly hysterical voice, somewhere between a whisper and a scream.

By now, my eyes were beginning to get their night vision and I could make out the figure of our TSM.

I suddenly started to enjoy this. It's not every day you get a Sergeant Major just where you want him.

'Bravo Oscar!' I said in a louder voice.

'I haven't got the new password,' he bleated pathetically.

I decided, reluctantly, to cut him some slack. Being a TSM, Geordie would have plenty of opportunities to make my life a misery if I pushed it too far.

'OK, sir... advance and be recognised.'

He approached my trench and instead of getting in and maybe getting dirt on his combats, he stood there like he was on the parade square, silhouetting himself nicely for any enemy snipers in the vicinity. He proceeded to spew out a load of verbal diarrhoea about the spares we needed and how we might be on the move soon, how the BC (Battery Commander) had apparently threatened to punch the BK (Battery Captain... you can't have two BCs so the latter is 'BK') if he didn't get his shiny arse from the comparative comfort of *HMS Fearless* and onto the islands. He then turned on his heel and marched off back to our admin area.

He didn't really need to be up here and he might at least have brought us up a hot brew with him. I hoped Quinny or someone else challenged him and he had to go through the embarrassment of not knowing the password again. Then again, he might do us all a favour and stay away.

The way it works is this. Gunner shoots Sergeant Major = murder. Sergeant Major shoots Gunner = idiot forgot password.

Unfortunately for 32 Alpha, he didn't stay away and we had a couple of nasty run-ins with our TSM.

Because our system was inoperative at night due to the lack of Blindfire, you were either on stag or trying to keep warm in your doss bag. We'd start chatting about our civvie lives, talking about what we'd be doing now if we'd never joined up. Bob bemoaned the fact he'd left the bakery in Halifax. I said I should have took my dad's advice and become an electrician with a trade behind me. Not one of us said we were glad that we'd joined the Army.

Funny, though: I loved it, in a masochistic sort of way, and I'd love the chance for 32 Alpha to meet up again one day, for the craic and a few beers, before we get too old.

As the war rolled slowly on, you got the feeling that we were winning. We didn't have the full picture, of course, but we'd seen nothing of the Argentinean Navy since the start, their extremely brave Air Force had taken the mother of all kicking's and their largely-conscript Army, while doing its best, was also being stuffed on the ground. Victory wasn't a certainty, but it was in sight.

There was always the feeling, though, that the scales could tip back the other way. The enemy had the power to hit us very hard, as they'd demonstrated a couple of days after they'd hit *Ardent* (incidentally, killing a 17-year-old sailor from my home town) when they came back after her sister ship, *HMS Antelope*.

The day she was attacked, the weather was OK. The 'tit-for-tat' battle of bomb alley, or 'Death Valley' if you were an Argie pilot, continued. Those who were still able to fight were full of courage and they were giving it their best shot.

The air raid warnings went off and there was a mad scramble for cover or weapons – our tracker head was on the blink again, so we were limited to our SLRs – and then a couple of Skyhawk's screamed overhead into a cloud of lead and other ordnance. *Antelope* was the pilots' target: she was stationed at the entrance to San Carlos water in a guard position, protecting our beach head. One of them was shot down immediately by a Rapier missile from another site, more in an ASM (air-to-surface missile) role than a SAM role because it was fired down from the hillside at the jet as it skimmed across the waves.

The second missed on his first run and dropped his bombs in the sea before getting back on his bike to the mainland. His decision was probably not made out of choice but from necessity; his Sky Hawk would have been down to the last dregs of aviation fuel and couldn't make another sweep. If he was lucky, and didn't bump into a sortie of Harriers on his return, he would just about have made it home.

Their mates weren't far behind them; several waves of Mirages and Sky Hawks roared in over the anchorage, dodging the flak as they came. All of them seemed to set their sights on the *Antelope*. One Sky Hawk zeroed in at mast height and was hit by 20 mm cannon shells fired from the ship's decks. All credit to the brave, mad bastard, he managed to get his 500lb bombs away before he actually collided with the mast and disintegrated in a ball of flame. Amazingly, the bombs didn't explode and neither did any dropped by any of the other planes. Only one British sailor had been killed and it looked like a miraculous escape. There was a fire on board but it looked under control and after a while we forgot about it.

Night descended and we got on with our duties of four hours on, four hours off. I was with Benny, I think, and it was dark and very quiet, when somebody suddenly switched on the lights. The *Antelope* had just exploded with an enormous blast like nothing I'd ever seen before. She was a fair way off in San Carlos Water but I could feel the heat wave up on the hill and I nearly fell over, more with shock than anything else, though the pressure wave was noticeable. All around, lads who'd been asleep woke up and that tells you something: a few little bangs weren't enough to rouse us now. A series of other explosions followed, turning the water and the surrounding hills red and orange, hell-like and glowing, as they reflected the flames. I thought I'd just witnessed the destruction of a ship and her entire crew and I felt sick to my stomach with the horror of it all.

What we didn't know at the time was that the ship had been evacuated and the explosion had been caused by a UXB (unexploded bomb) going off and setting off a chain of explosions in her magazines. A very brave team of Royal Engineer bomb disposal experts, led by a Staff Sergeant James Prescott, were working to defuse it on board. Apparently, SSgt Prescott had extracted the bomb's fuse twice but each time had second thoughts and put it back. He took it out a third time and the bomb detonated, killing him instantly and taking an arm from one of his team. The eventual blast, which came some time later and peeled the frigate apart like a cheap sardine tin, created one of the most dramatic photographs of the war, and a permanent image in my head.

The hulk glowed throughout the night as we watched, numb and in shock. We tried to mask our feelings, as soldiers do. I remember someone saying, 'Oh well, a least we've got the warmth of a good fire!' to general cackles of amusement. You tend to make light of things in times of great stress but it was very forced. I felt an added sadness; the *Antelope* was one of the ships who had escorted us the seven or eight thousand miles down her and I remembered catching a glimpse of her one day in the rough South Atlantic seas from the deck of the *Geraint*.

At first light, we all gathered and watched the death throes of a once proud ship. She was defiant to the end, burning until there was nothing left to burn, just a mass of tangled molten metal. She finally succumbed to the inevitable and her back broke, sending her sliding to an icy grave in the Atlantic, engulfed in a volcanic mountain of steam.

I felt like saying a few words.

Bob said them for me: 'Quinny, you're in the seat, Benny, check the weapons. Let's get these fucking T's and A's done.' He pointed to the bubbling sea. 'Try and stop that happening again.'

We all went about our business waiting for the next 'Air Raid Warning Red'.

* * * * *

In between the Argentine air force trying to kill us, and the Para Gunners joining in when the mood took them, our TSM continued to piss us all off.

A Royal Marine tracked vehicle became bogged down near our position. Geordie must have seen it, because he marched up to the Marines and offered his services. Or rather, the services of 32 Alpha. We had been having a reasonable day up to the point of his arrival. It was probably someone's birthday probably mine I had my twentieth there, because we were celebrating with a tin of fruitcake and some extra boiled sweets and choccie.

Events unfolded something like this.

Enter stage right: TSM, sporting bulled boots, ironed combats, shiny cap badge – the full parade ground look, the absolute dog's bollocks, with SMG slung on back to complete the 'ready for anything' look.

'Ah, Sergeant,' he says to Bob. 'I've got a quick job for you and your lads.'

'Yes, Sir, what's that then?'

'There's a Royal Marine vehicle bogged in down the hill. I want you to get your one tonner and go down and winch it out.'

Pregnant Pause.

'You're fucking kidding, aren't you?'

'No, I'm not, Sergeant. It won't take long if we all lend a hand.'

'Look, Geordie, if you want to winch them out, go and do it with a THQ vehicle. You expect me to totally decamp my position and leave myself open to air attack? We're at war, not some exercise on Otterburn ranges.'

'Listen, Sergeant, I'm not asking you, I'm ordering you.'

'No, you listen, Sergeant Major. You can fuck right off. I'm not doing it.'

'Do you realise, Sergeant, I could have you court-martialled for this.'

'Go on then, court martial me. You never know, the charge might be murder.'

Geordie took the hint, and stormed off in a rage.

32 Alpha – 1, TSM – 0.

We won that battle, thanks to Bob sticking to his guns.

The TSM was having a giraffe: he was living in a farm building, with nice, hot water and fresh rations every day, and would periodically appear up at our position and start telling us to have a shave and polish our boots. That sort of crap may have worked in Aden or Malaya, in an old fashioned field gun Battery, but it was way out of line in San Carlos.

From then on, I always had a greater respect for Bob. He was a soldier's soldier, and it was nice to see him later rise to the rank of Warrant Officer Second Class SMIG (Sergeant Major Instructor Of Gunnery). I'm sure he put a few cocky Sergeants in their place over the years and he may have blacked a few careless NIG eyes in the tank hangar, too.

The pace of the war was gathering momentum, heading towards a climax, and the Argentine forces looked as though they might be about to throw in the towel. We received orders to prepare to move. The Welsh Guards of 5 Brigade were being shifted from San Carlos Water to Bluff Cove, much closer to Stanley, to assist with the final stages of the ground war. We would be tasked to give them air defence cover, while they waited to come ashore, then during the transfer and, finally, once they had landed.

We were to travel aboard the Royal Fleet Auxiliary ship *Sir Galahad*, with other troops accompanying us on her sister *Sir Tristram*. The idea was that we would be helicoptered aboard late in the day and set off at dusk. That way, we would travel and arrive under cover of darkness and the *Galahad* could drop us all off and be back at San Carlos by dawn.

I was glad we were going to be on the move again. I was sick of getting bombed and watching ships sink at San Carlos. I might as well get bombed and watch ships sink somewhere else.

But I was surprised that 32 Alpha had been given this important task. The continuing problems with our Rapier system meant that the cover we could provide would be unreliable at best; I would have thought that the top brass would have wanted the best kit protecting their men. These things cannot – or should not – be left to chance.

STILL WATCHING MEN BURN

As it turned out, 32 Alpha was just a number of spanners thrown in the works, the first couple having been lobbed right at the start.

First, we were late boarding and didn't set off until five hours behind schedule. This was good in one way, because it meant we went aboard during hours of darkness which made us all feel a lot safer. But the downside of this was that we would arrive at the other end after dawn, in daylight.

Second, because of the delay, the ship was sailing to Port Pleasant, Fitzroy, an inlet three or four miles closer to where we were setting off from, and a two- or three-hour march overland to Bluff Cove. But no-one told the Welsh Guards about the change of destination.

Right from the start, I had a bad feeling about being at sea again. It was only a couple of weeks since I'd seen the *Antelope* go up like a arsonist's dream; that had been utterly horrific to watch, and a sick feeling spread through my guts as we went aboard the *Sir Galahad*.

The Guardsmen didn't seem to share my concern. In fact, I was astounded by their nonchalance. Apart from their uniform, they acted like they were on a P&O cruise to the Caribbean. It wasn't their fault; as members of 5 Brigade, they hadn't yet witnessed the sudden and terrible ferocity of a successful air attack.

We must have looked pretty rough and we probably stank, too; anyway, we got some funny looks from the Welsh lads as we paced up and down nervously, like cats in a Chinese take-away. They gave us a wide berth at first; they didn't know who we were, as we weren't wearing any head-dress, and probably thought we were Special Forces. But as soon as they worked out that we were just RA dogsbodies, one of their officers ordered us to grab mops and buckets and start scrubbing the boat from top to bottom, washing out the bogs and all. At least it gave us something to think about and focus on.

After an hour or so of that, and making the most of the unfamiliar warmth of my surroundings, I fell asleep, my exhaustion overcoming my fear as the throb of the engines lulled me away. A couple of hours later I woke up, hot and clammy, and peeled some of the layers of my clothing off. The stale smell of sweat, dirt and weeks-old underwear hit me like a slap in the face: I was right, I *did* stink. I took advantage of the hot pipes to dry some of my kit, change my socks and scrape some of the crap off my boots so I could polish them.

Not long after that, we pulled into 'Port Pleasant', which wasn't particularly well-named and dropped anchor.

It was June 8.

It was dawn alright, and not just any old dawn, either: the weather had been cloudy and squally in recent days, a real bonus because that restricted enemy air activity. Today, the sky was bright and clear and blue – horribly right for air attack.

I made my way up on deck at this time, getting myself on stag with the Rapier, standing next to our kit in the cargo nets.

It felt very like the day we'd arrived in San Carlos Water, when I'd been up top wondering where the opposition were, and when they'd suddenly arrived. I looked around. We were anchored in a narrow channel, bobbing gently on an almost flat-calm sea, with the greeny-grey hills of the Falklands overlooking us. Sheep grazed unconcerned on the heather a mile or two away and the only sound was the slap of the gentle swell on the ship's hull, the low thrum of the idling engines and the screech of seagulls riding the breeze above us.

If I was writing a bad thriller, I'd probably say it was 'ominously quiet'.

You could see for miles in the crystal clear air. I was very nervous. Actually, scratch that: I was shitting bricks. I felt sick right down in my guts, and I strained to hear the roar of approaching turbines. I was sure – absolutely convinced – that we would be visited by our South American friends very soon and that we needed to get moving; otherwise they were going to find us sitting around like toy boats in a pond.

The phrase 'sitting ducks' is one of the most overused there is. But it applied absolutely to us at that point. We were anchored up around two hundred yards from shore in great visibility. There was no escort travelling with us, and no anti-aircraft capability aboard either boat to speak of, just a couple of Bofors guns. The Welsh Guards had offered to defend us with their machine guns – which would have been better than nothing – but this offer had been rejected by the captain of the *Sir Galahad*. I think he thought Rapier and air combat patrols were providing cover, but we were the Rapier, we were still aboard and we were malfunctioning anyway, as were others. Additionally, we had no Harrier support because a strip at San Carlos had been damaged by a crash landing and was temporarily out of service. The nearest Harriers were operating from *HMS Hermes*, kept far out to sea for safety reasons, and that and the fact they had plenty of other jobs to do rendered them ineffective, too. Add to this the fact that we were nice and close to the Argentinean positions, so they would surely be getting on the blower as we sat there and you begin to see our predicament.

Oh, well. We'd be getting off, soon.

But we didn't. We just stayed put. It seemed like we were waiting there for hours. It was blindingly obvious to me that it wasn't a question of whether we would be attacked, just when it would happen and how bad it would be. The longer we waited, the nearer it got.

Not long after we dropped anchor, a guy called Major Ewen Southby-Tailyour came aboard. A few years earlier, he had been in command of the Royal Marine detachment stationed on the islands and he knew every cove and crag of the place like the back of his hand. He also knew we were extremely vulnerable to air attack so he had commandeered a couple of landing craft and was desperate for the Welsh Guards officers to get their guys off the ship. But they refused. Apparently, they didn't want to mix men and ammunition in the same boats and, anyway, they couldn't understand why we couldn't just sail the three or four miles round the corner to the original destination, Bluff Cove. Why should their guys have to get their boots all muddy marching over the hill?

Like their soldiers, I guess they knew that an air attack was possible. They just hadn't *seen* one; they didn't know how quickly it could happen, or how awful, how horrible, it could be. Why would they? They'd spent their war out at sea on the QE2 to this point.

It was probably already too late. As these conversations were going on, an Argentine observation post on nearby Mount Harriet had seen us and got on the radio to the Argentine air force on the mainland. At that point, a lot of young Welsh Guards were already dead men.

They didn't know that, and they still seemed totally relaxed – watching cartoons on the telly, playing cards, having a laugh and a joke. They must have thought I was nuts, wired to the eyeballs will stress and adrenalin.

Every minute, my heart rate increased.

I started to sweat heavily, despite the cold, and my mouth was dry as sandpaper.

I scanned the horizon constantly: *Where's the fucking choppers? Let's get off this tub, quick.*

I wanted to shout and scream at someone to pull their finger out.

But we sat there for what seemed like a lifetime, and still nothing happened.

My old religious hypocrisy returned: I remembered I had a 'Miraculous Medal' in my combat jacket pocket. It was silver and about the size of an old half-pence piece, with a picture of the Virgin Mary on it. I opened the flap of my pocket to get the medal out for good luck, and put my hand inside.

Nothing.

Oh shit, where's it at?

I searched in all of my pockets – gone.

I've had it. It's a sign. I'm going to die.

Don't be daft, you wanker, it can't help you.

Yes it can.

Where the fuck is it? Excuse my language, God.

Suddenly, I realised that it was in my other jacket, which was in my large pack under the cargo net. I raced to the net and started searching through all of the kit, tearing at it frantically until I found my pack. I was in a state of panic now, as I fiddled with the straps and buckles, thinking, *I'm bound to hear our choppers coming any second to take us off, and everyone on board will be looking at me tangled up in the netting like some demented crab dressed in camouflage.*

Or will I hear Argentine jet engines?

I found the medal. *Thank you, Lord.*

I relaxed, slightly.

I've got everything now, I'm ready to go.

And what happened? Still nothing.

I thought back to old war movies; the troops always seemed to have a sense of urgency.

I remembered the great Arnhem film *A Bridge Too Far*, the bit where the Polish Paras are paddling like crazy to get across the river before they're seen by the Germans.

Of course, they are seen and nearly all of them perish in the water under raking Spandau fire.

Well, that was a cheerful thought. But not to worry... we're the British. We're the experts at warfare, we've been doing this sort of thing for centuries, all over the world, since the days of wooden galleons and before, and we've stuffed everybody, everywhere. We've done the French, we've done the Germans, we've done the Spanish... we used to rule the entire bloody world. We know what we're doing, we know what's what. We aren't scared of a few fucking Argentineans.

Yeah, right. Bollocks. Please, some bastard with a few pips on his shoulder, make a decision. I can see what's coming and I'm a little nobody gunner. Why can't you?

At last Bob and the rest of our lads appeared on deck and told me to get ready to move. Someone must have pressed the bell: we were getting off the bus.

Thank fucking *fuck* for that.

I remember Quinny and Benny moaning because they'd missed the end of *Bugs Bunny*. Well, at least the Guards got to watch it all, the poor bastards.

I could hear the comforting *wop, wop, wop* of rotor blades echoing around the hills and we quickly lined up in our chalk. After hooking the launcher up to the first chopper, we jumped on board the second for a quick two- or three-minute jaunt to *terra firma*.

Even on a short flight like that one, the heat inside the aircraft starts to make you sleepy, especially as a major adrenalin surge starts to die off. I lay there, feeling comfortable and warm. I didn't want to get off, back out onto the cold, soggy ground around Fitzroy; I wanted to stay in this roaring, shaking metal womb for the rest of my days.

But sadly, and all too soon, the nose of the chopper lifted and we sank to the ground; it was time to get out, from the oven back into the fridge.

We found ourselves in the middle of the Maroon Machine: 2 Para.

They were awaiting orders for the final push on Stanley. The Paras are a unique group of fighting men who hate all soldiers who don't wear their famous red beret. Even though we were on their side, and our missiles could (in theory) protect them from air attack, we were still crap-hats, sub standard-military scum in their eyes…almost worse even than the Argies: at least they gave them a fight. If it was a choice between a British Para giving his last cigarette to a wounded British crap hat or a wounded Argentinean Paratrooper who'd just killed half of his mates, you can bet he would favour the Argie. It's the airborne brotherhood; they stick together.

They weren't particularly pleasant to work alongside but they had my respect, that's for sure. They were our shock troops, the soldiers any Army needs to win wars. Thoroughly professional, they did not know the meaning of the word 'defeat'.

As soon as the choppers dropped the Rapier off, we got into action as fast as we could. The Paras eyed us with suspicious curiosity as we ran around with cables and equipment, like ants on speed. There was one huge West Indian lad in a trench watching us hats scuttle about. I remember thinking he must have taken some stick to get through P Coy, the airborne selection course. Anybody will tell you (who has served) that racism is unfortunately rife in the Army. But he was no longer a black man, he was now maroon. The guys alongside him would have died for him. I knew better, but some of our lads tried to make conversation with the cherry berets, only to be met with a glare saying, *'Fuck off, hat, this is my war.'*

After about fifteen minutes, we were up and running and starting to test and adjust the system to make sure it was functioning correctly. Even as I looked through the optics at the *Galahad* I could see that nothing was moving on board. She and the *Tristram* must have been at anchor for hours by now. I couldn't understand, for the life of me, why they weren't getting the lads off.

We passed 32 Alpha's T's and A's but we weren't happy. That persistent, intermittent tracker head problem was still there and I kept hearing the systems fault tone in my head-set. This is a knocking sound, like a woodpecker tapping at a tree. Once you hear this sound, you know that your hi-tech weapon system will not work: it is nothing more than a lump of very expensive scrap metal. It was tremendously frustrating; one minute, everything seemed to be working fine, the next the deadly knocking in your ears.

But there was nothing to be done till the REME boys were able to get to us. We'd just have to do the best we could. I looked around our position. Once again, there was no cover. We were totally windswept and stuck out like tits on a bull.

As I write this, I find myself drifting back to that day, nearly 25 years ago. I feel uneasy, sick, jumpy – just as I did then. I was very frightened, basically. The whole day had been too quiet and uneventful; even the Paras were taking it easy, grabbing the opportunity to sort their kit out, clean their rifles and get some scoff down their throats. 32 Alpha was the only real air defence cover and that knocking tone in my ear just wouldn't go away for long.

It was just after 1300hrs. Aboard the *Galahad* and the *Tristram*, half a mile away on the flat, grey sea, the Hooray Henries were finally coming to a decision as to how to disembark.

Several hours after arriving.

The sky was clear and the weak, wintry sun was hanging by a thread somewhere above the horizon. Off in the distance, there would have been the noise of the ongoing battle, but I didn't really notice it: the only sound was the low chat of the nearby Paras and, closer, the other members of 32 Alpha, the keening of seabirds wheeling overhead and the flap and slap of my smock as the wind tugged at it.

Around 1400hrs, I was tracking visually around the valleys, then out to sea, looking for any enemy activity, when my heart missed a beat.

I could clearly see a Sky Hawk heading right for the ships. Then I saw more.

'Bogies, incoming,' I yelled, and all hell broke loose as the lads around me sprang into action.

At this point, I could not hear the noise of the jet engines. Usually we'd receive the urgent message 'Air Raid Warning Red' sent by Battery command post on the radio, although on this occasion I don't remember hearing it. It later transpired that a vital radar system operated for us by Chile was down for essential maintenance work: just another dodgy roll of the dice for the lads aboard the *Galahad*.

The Skyhawk's were making their way at low level to the large, grey sitting ducks wallowing in the sound below me; the other lads had sprung into action, Bob by my side, more missiles being readied. The Paras were starting to stand up and a few had already begun firing their rifles and machine guns.

I concentrated on the lead jet; I had the cross-hairs smack bang in the middle of him.

'Target, tracking, in cover.'

Bob screamed 'Engage!'

'Firing!'

I pressed the fire button with my left-hand index-finger.

Nothing.

Except that horrible, familiar woodpecker, tapping on a tree in my bone-dome.

I pressed again, and again, and again.

All I got was that tap, tap, tap, drowned out, now, by the screech of their engines, rolling over the water and off the hills towards us.

The attack came and went in the blink of an eye.

The lead Skyhawk's two 250kg high explosive bombs hit the *Sir Galahad* and exploded with devastating effect. The second pilot missed, his bombs sending huge fountains of water crashing over the flames as they detonated in the sea, but the third A4 hit the target, adding to the inferno. The air was full of the sound of ear-piercing explosions, jet engines and the unearthly howling of the nearby Paras, screaming in fury at the Argentineans and unloading thousands of rounds of GMPG and rifle fire in their wake.

By the grace of God, the bombs that had hit the *Tristram* had failed to explode, though two men were killed by them, but the *Galahad* was already well ablaze; in a twisted irony, she was carrying a large quantity of petrol for Rapier generators and this and the ammunition aboard were a lethal combination.

Soldiers were jumping into the water, their clothes on fire, as others ran around on the deck trying to get off. As the carnage unfolded in front of me, I could do nothing but stand there, watching men burn.

It was unreal, somehow, as though I was at the cinema, watching a war film. I remember looking at Bob, standing up helplessly by the tracker, as the Paras turned their anger on us, screaming and shouting obscenities.

'You fucking crap hat bastards, why didn't you fire your fucking missiles?'

'Wankers!'

'Twats… why didn't you shoot the fuckers down?'

How do you explain that it wasn't our fault? That a fuse had blown, or the computer had crashed, or some 50p pin had got bent out of shape somewhere – that 32 Alpha should never have been here in the first place, and that the boys should never have been left their sitting on the boats anyway? Seven hours spent playing cards and watching cartoons, as they waited to die.

The Paras, and the Scots Guards who were not far away, had run down to the water line to help with the casualties who were starting to come ashore in lifeboats. Many of them were obviously terribly injured. We couldn't go; we had to stay with our useless sodding Rapier and its pointless bloody missiles and, anyway, I didn't want to go. I felt awful. I'd been in the hot seat but had been unable to do anything to stop the attack.

Oddly, as I sat transfixed in shock, watching the *Galahad* burn and explode, someone stuck a mess tin of food on my knee.

I couldn't eat.

I was still shaking and shit-scared and selfishly convinced that we were going to die, too: more planes were sure to arrive in a minute, and we couldn't even defend ourselves with our kit knackered. All seemed lost.

I just wanted to get out of the seat and into a trench and bury my head in the mud. I shouted to Ricky, the NIG of the sub, 'Ricky, do us a favour, I'm getting cramp in my leg and I want to go and eat my scoff. Take over, will you?'

Ricky didn't mind too much. He didn't know he was about to shoot down his first aircraft. I jumped out, Ricky jumped in, and I headed for the nearest trench, put my tin lid on and started to ram my scoff down my throat. I'd just shovelled the first lump of stew into my mouth, fighting a feeling of nausea, when I heard the noise of death, a screaming jet engine heading our way.

Where the fuck is it?

The noise seemed to be coming from the sea. Wrong. It was another Sky Hawk, right behind us and then streaking directly overhead, banking as it did so. I could clearly read the words 'Armada' on the white fuselage and see the pilot's helmet.

Bob stood in the open and bravely spun the tracker head around after the receding jet, as I watched tracer rounds from the Paras machine guns flashing uncomfortably close to his head , which continued banking to the left, towards the sea, and then turned inland again, starting to come back towards us. He must have seen us and decided to come back and finish us off. We were all firing our rifles at the jet every round we had, just a token defensive gesture as we sat there waiting to be incinerated, when, suddenly… *Whoosh!*... a Rapier missile streaked off the beam towards the Sky Hawk. It veered left and right, looking unstable, before it gathered itself and went in true on course.

'Get the bastard, Ricky!'

The pilot saw it coming and put his foot on the brake, banking hard to the right to evade the missile.

Too slow Jose… fuck off! Bang! Direct hit.

He was hit plum centre and crashed into the mountainside in a huge fireball, as though he had been carrying napalm. Good job the bastard didn't drop it on his first run.

At least this action saved us a bit of face and even the remaining Paras must have appreciated it, as the abuse came a little quieter now.

On the burning ship below us, a total of 48 men had been killed – 32 Welsh Guardsmen, eleven other Army personnel and five RFA crewmen, with many more badly burned and wounded. Among them, famously, was Simon Weston. It was the worst single loss of life in the war, and the worst, indeed, since the Second World War.

Six Royal Marines died in a landing craft later on, too.

For what felt like hours, I sat in my trench and watched, mesmerised, as the helicopter pilots called in to pluck more survivors from the burning hulk became the heroes of the hour. Their flying was breathtaking: they flew blind through clouds of choking black smoke, their rotor blades practically touching the burning side of the ship, to lift casualties off. It was an awesome display of bravery and skill, especially in light of the potential for more air attacks at any moment.

Gradually, the feelings of fear and shock ebbed away and the relief at still being alive myself overcame everything, bringing with it a kind of euphoria. It was quite bizarre: for a while, I didn't feel cold, hungry, lonely, scared, tired, and pissed off or anything negative. It was like being immortal, just for a while.

After half an hour or so, though, it was state normal. All that shit flooded back into my brain and body and I started moaning, as you do. *'I'm bloody freezing, it's shite, the Falklands are shite, this war's shite someone shout end -ex please'*

The clear sky had clouded over and, an hour too late, it started to snow. In June. Now we had something else to gripe about, the carnage of the day was temporarily forgotten, locked away deep inside my mind.

Bob got on the blower and demanded a couple of intelligent crap hats from the REME. 32 Alpha was next to useless, and it needed a tonic – a gentle massage of its circuitry by the elegant, piano-playing fingers of the techs. The kit had to work. It wasn't so much of a case of us losing face any more – it was more about losing our heads, legs and arms. Eventually, the REME emerged through the snow, like Robocops with toolboxes and very high foreheads. They asked Bob to make the patient safe and administered an electronic Lemsip, told us to keep her wrapped up and if she didn't show any signs of shooting down aircraft in the morning to give them another call and they would have to operate.

We waved them bye-bye and copied one another by shivering and swearing. The Paras started to copy us by shivering as well, only their shivering was more hard, like airborne shivering, not your bog standard crap hat shivering.

As night fell, we switched to our normal routine – food, sentry duty and sleep. It sounds harsh, but life had to go on. It's no use crying over burnt Guardsmen, and we didn't. Though it would eventually hit me hard, very hard – terrible feelings of guilt, sobbing tears, horrific flashbacks, wishing I'd died out there myself – my mind had shut down those emotions for the time being. We had survived our last major action of the war.

IT SMELLS LIKE VICTORY

For me, the last few nights of the war were spent huddled in my trench watching the fireworks on the hillsides around me as the final battles unfolded. I'd sip my mug of tea, hands wrapped round it for warmth, watching our tracer rounds go up the mountain and the Argie tracer rounds coming back down. From this distance, it all looked quite safe and jolly, like some sort of video game or Bonfire Night show: it was only many years after the war, when I read books about famous battles at places like Wireless Ridge, Mount Longdon, Tumbledown and Goose Green, fought and won against overwhelming numerical odds, that I realised how lucky I had been to have joined the Royal Artillery. I was a soldier, and I fought in the Falklands, but I had no understanding of the primal, eternal savagery of warfare that had been going on around me. I had no comprehension of the loss of life that was occurring. A few miles from where I sat, just a Sunday afternoon stroll away, men with families, with wives and kids, were lying dead, their heads blown apart. Others were holding their guts in, watching themselves bleed to death. Still others, full of shrapnel, or dismembered by artillery, or stuck through the throat with a bayonet, were finding different ways to die.

I respected our elite regiments then, but that respect has grown over time. The Paras, Marines and Guardsmen did the hard graft, tabbing, yomping, staggering, killing and being killed all the way to the insignificant little pile of wooden houses which constituted Port Stanley, the capital of the Falkland Islands, and victory. In doing so, they continued the tradition of British soldiers throughout the history of our Army: they won because their training was first rate, because they were hard men and because they believed in each other. Regiments like the Paras and the Scots Guards, and the Royal Marine Commandos, are much more of a family than a large outfit like the Royal Artillery. They look out for each other even years later, when they become civilians; their commitment, will-to-win and togetherness on the battlefield was what pulled them through. Compared to these units, our contribution seemed minor but when you think of the damage a fighter bomber could have caused to the Task Forces it puts it into context. We'd done our best and that's all anyone can ask for. We might be the crap hat, long-range snipers of the Royal Regiment of Artillery, but we'd played our part and no doubt saved lives.

Dawn came on the 14th June, and we heard reports that there were white flags flying over Stanley. I can't remember how I actually felt: I must have been extremely happy, knowing that there was a good chance of me getting home in one piece now, but I do know we weren't running around shouting or hugging each other. For one thing, I don't think we really believed it was the end. We had to be vigilant in case the Argie Air Force decided that they weren't going to surrender just yet. There was a lot of radio traffic batting to and fro, and the rumour control centre was churning out its usual bull. However, before long the order came through: cease firing.

Happy days: it was official.

Things were definitely more relaxed now, and I set off on a wander around Fitzroy, admiring the wildlife. I decided to celebrate the surrender by shooting a duck. We plucked it, cut its head off and then cooked it over a wood fire, tummies rumbling and saliva dripping from our gobs. I was really looking forward to a nice, juicy slice of 'Duck à la Fitzroy' but unfortunately it tasted like the sole of an Army boot. Well, I'm no slop jockey.

For some reason, the powers that be got us back on the *Galahad* to move salvaged stores and equipment (she'd been smoking for a while but the fires were pretty much out now; she would later be towed out to sea and sunk as a war grave). This was typical British Army stuff. War ends – sweeping up shite begins. Being handed this crap detail only confirmed my long-held impression that the rest of the Army thought we had the word 'twat' stamped on our foreheads. *Quo fas et gloria ducunt* was our motto; roughly translated into English, as far as I could see it meant: 'Oh look, there's some RA wankers, let's get them to do all the crap jobs.'

Well, I was determined to get something out of this – stolen goodies, beer, fags, whatever, but more than anything I wanted a shower. I could have killed for one. I think Scouse Kilty was with me as we gave the NCO the slip and went below deck. It was weird being back on board and walking around this death ship. We found the toilets and the showers and, fuck it, I quickly stripped off my minging kit. I threw my last pair of shreddies at the bulkhead and watched them slide down the wall like a rotting pizza before they dissolved on the floor. The water was still on – I assume it was gravity-fed – and I jumped in, happily scraping the crap off. I didn't have any soap or shampoo but it felt good, if chilly. I was even having a little sing to myself when the door crashed open and in walked two monkeys. You know the type: *I want a red beret, but I can't hack P Coy, so I'll join the RMP*. And why do these tossers always ask you obvious questions: 'What the fuck do you think you're on?'

'Er, I'm on the *Galahad*.'

'Yes, but what do you think you're doing?'

'I'm having a shower.'

'Get your fucking arse out of there now! What's your name, rank and number?'

I got out of the shower, started to dry myself and told them who I was. One of them started giving be a rollicking – the ship was still burning, it was a war grave so this was sacrilege, didn't I know there was still ammunition on board and my life could be in danger. It wasn't like I'd asked to go aboard, but I gave him the respect he wanted by calling him Corporal and they both went away.

I got dressed, used the head and re-joined the RA chain gang.

That shower was a sign of better times to come, as we all started to behave like kids in a toy shop. All squaddies are really big kids, with a love of mischief and a fascination for things that go bang. I think it was about the last day at Fitzroy that I heard a machine gun firing nearby. Instead of running home to Bob, we decided to investigate.

'Fuck me, mate, look at that.'

On the beach, next to a large pile of ammunition, there was a group of Royal Marines letting rip into the sea with all kinds of pyrotechnics. We cautiously approached, being careful to look as British as we possibly could. One lad was on the ground, firing a GPMG into the sea; the ammunition belt went on forever, rattling out of a sea of boxes as the rounds were pulled through the breech. I waited for a break in the firing but the Marines just kept changing the barrels when they started to glow with the heat. Luckily, eventually there was a stoppage. As the firer cleared it, I spoke up.

'All right lads, OK if we have a cabbie?'

The Marines turned around as one and suspiciously eyed us up and down, noting that we were wearing no berets.

'What unit are you with?' asked the biggest one, in a fairly hostile tone.

There was a chance we might be Paras, I guess. They would have loved nothing more than to share the ammunition with their airborne friends, though in more of a friendly-fire sort of way.

'RA mate. We're Air Defence.'

They seemed to relax a bit. 'OK lads fill your boots, there's plenty for everyone, roll up, roll up, see if you can win a teddy.'

This was the most fun-packed hour of my military career – a huge lucky dip of death. I grabbed a wooden box of grenades from the pile and started pulling the pins and throwing them into the sea. It reminded me of the old black and white World War II naval films, when a U boat is being depth charged: a dull thud, followed by a huge fountain of water and then a load of dead fish floating to the surface. Banzai, they should have recorded this for an

Army recruitment film… *the* most fun you can *possibly* have with your clothes on. And no more far-fetched than some NIG wind surfing off the Bahamas. A box of grenades later, and a few hundred South Atlantic marine creatures floating about, we moved onto a box of 66mm anti-tank weapons. I'd never fired one before, but the instructions were on the side. It was a bang and bin weapon, a bit like the girls in sunny Scunny, only you didn't have to spend all night throwing drinks at a 66. The Marines had found an interesting figure 11 target to fire at. Not the usual shape of an ugly, commie bastard infantry man; no, this was slightly bigger and had the words *RFA Sir Galahad* painted on the side. I watched as they hosing the ship down, wondering whether any bastard was stupid enough to be having a shower on board. The instructions for the 66 were something like 'extend to full length, pull out safety pin, flip sights up, aim, press fire button and away you go'. Only the Yanks could be responsible for a bit of kit like that.

Whoosh!

Off shot the round, spinning through the air before exploding in the water to the stern of the *Galahad*.

After having a cabbie on the gimpy, we said farewell to our Royal Navy pals and left them fighting over the last few 66s.

On reflection, of course, firing at the *Galahad* so soon after the dreadful loss of life aboard her was more than a little insensitive. But she was there, and she wasn't going anywhere ever again. As I say, I thought about this sort of thing much more deeply later on.

On our arrival back at the detachment, Bob was there to greet us.

'Where have you two wankers been?'

'Oh, we had to give some Marines some help moving some ammo.'

Not exactly a lie, when you think about it.

'Well, it's nice of you to come and do your bit for the RA. Get your shit together. Mack, go and relieve Platsy, we're getting ready to move by chopper.'

We soon had all the kit packed to be transported by air to the big end-ex piss up. A couple of Sea Kings arrived, and we hooked up the launcher and the missiles and nets with our personal kit. Then they disappeared, still hugging the landscape en route to Stanley in case some rogue

Mirage pilot decided to take Rapier on at his level. Even though the kit didn't always work, and though an official ceasefire had been declared, I still felt extremely vulnerable without it. We hadn't waited long when out of nowhere came the large fuselage of a Chinook, circling over Fitzroy. There were a few lame jokes about hoping it was one of ours, and not an enemy one stuffed with Argie Marines, or worse still, pilots who were going to have a go now that we were Rapierless. It hovered above our position and I could make out a Union Jack on its side. I soon wished it would fuck off again as its twin rotors blasted us with grass and sheep shit in the down draft.

It landed, we got on board, it took off, and I fell asleep. Well, that's the effect helicopters have on me.

We landed at Port Stanley and someone woke me up. It was certainly a sight for sore eyes. The Argentineans had completely trashed the place. The streets were covered in debris of all descriptions – weapons, clothing, abandoned vehicles, faeces.

There's a great scene in perhaps the ultimate war film, *Apocalypse Now*. Colonel Kilgore, the Stetson-wearing lunatic who surfs while Charlie tries to machine gun him, is explaining how he loves the smell of napalm in the morning. It smells like victory, he says.

No it doesn't. Victory smells mainly of excrement.

Everywhere you looked lay little piles of the stuff. At first, I assumed the locals must have had a lot of dogs, and badly-trained dogs at that. But a closer inspection revealed some of the mounds had toilet paper stuck on the top, and I'd never met a hound that could wipe its own backside. It was quite obvious that there were only three groups of people that could be responsible.

Number one, the Islanders.

Number two, the British Army.

Number three, the Argentineans.

We soon found out that group three were responsible. It needed cleaning up, but not to worry, the RA get all the crap jobs. There wasn't a lot of joking on that particular detail.

The only way that I can describe the scene in Stanley was one of organised anarchy. Everyone was so chuffed to have made it this far that we all just got smashed and let our now slightly-longer hair down – even the Officers. Our troop was accommodated in an abandoned weather station. I say abandoned because there was no-one there when we claimed it, but someone had left not long before and they had helpfully left their little brown calling cards to prove it.

Everyone suddenly had an extra weapon, usually a Belgian-made Argie FN. Bored with our SLRs, we sat around stripping and re-assembling our new toys. Once your rifle is cleaned, the natural thing was to go and fire it. I gave Scouse Denmark from 31 Delta a folding stock FN and suggested we go whack off a few rounds. We found some old Argie bunkers littered with bits of kit and thousands of rounds of 7.62mm ammo and spent a happy half hour, minding our own business, blasting off mag after mag on fully automatic. It's nearly impossible to control an FN whilst firing on auto – it rears up into the air, nearly knocking you onto your backside – but it's good fun. No boring NCOs telling you to keep your weapon pointed down the range ('For inspection, port arms, blah, blah, blah…').

In between changing mags and rubbing the mud off the loose rounds we found on the floor, we heard, 'Oi, you two, what do you think you're doing?' We turned around,

keeping our weapons pointed at the bunker, and saw some
fat Sergeant we didn't recognise stomping towards us. He
made us come to attention – can you believe it, we had two
loaded assault rifles, he was unarmed and there was no-one
about. He must have been pissed up, pay corps or on an
ego trip; he gave us a bollocking, took out his little pocket
book and pencil and asked for our names and Regiment.
We gave him names and Batteries. He ordered us to unload
and confiscated our FNs and we headed back to the
weather station, hoping that he would follow up the names
that we had given him, as both were in 9 Battery and were
rather Afro-Caribbean in appearance. He could have asked
to have seen our dog tags, but his real motive was
obviously our FNs. None of that mattered though: on
arrival back at our new base we discovered Father
Christmas had been. Most of our troop were stood around
some wooden crates that were full of brand spanking new
FN rifles, still in their grease-proof paper. We were just
too late; they'd all been claimed, and their proud new
owners were sat there drooling and caressing them like a
shapely pair of legs in some black fishnet stockings. Not to
worry. I did what all good, senior Gunners do and found

someone to take advantage of. At the far end of the room sat a Gunner with a new FN. Edmo was not the keenest of soldiers. He'd probably set off to go to the chip shop and ended up in the Army by accident. If Belgium went to the trouble of making such a fine weapon I felt it was only right that its owner should have an idea which end the round came out.

'How's it going, Edmo?'

'All right, man,' he said, looking up at me in suspicion.

'Let's have a look at your FN.'

'Fuck off, no way; you won't give us it back, man.'

'I will. Listen, I'll give you a Mars bar if you let me fire it.'

The fool agreed.

'Howay man, where's the Mars bar?'

'As soon as we get back to England I'll get you a Mars bar infact you can have two, Edmo, I promise.' And I spent the rest of the afternoon back at our illegal range.

The euphoria of victory and survival soon started to wear off and we were rapidly getting pissed off with alternately cleaning up Stanley or sitting around doing pretty much nothing. Some of the task force had already set sail for home and it now looked like we'd be the last to leave. Whenever I hear the song *Stairway to Heaven* by Led Zeppelin I am transported back in time to that old work shop. Taff Blenkin was the only one in our Troop with a Walkman and I think he only had one tape, which happened to be a Led Zep thing. It was good to get snuggled down inside my doss bag, put the headset on and try to forget where I was for a while.

To keep our morale up we continued playing with the equipment left strewn around by the enemy. The Argies had 'Roland' surface-to-air missile systems and I came across some of our lads vandalising one, smashing the electronics with metal bars and rocks. Thommo decided to do it in style by firing a full mag of 7.62mm into it with his trendy folding stock FN. We were all standing round giggling when we got the fright of our lives: some of the rounds must have ignited a missile because all of a sudden one shot out, with a large bang and a cloud of smoke. It roared into the air about a hundred feet before spiralling back down to earth and exploding not far away, showering us with dirt. It was a mad thing to do, really, and gives you some insight into our mental state. I often wonder what would have happened if the Roland had hit one of our helicopters, perhaps one being flown by Prince Andrew? A story of old is that a Gunner from T Battery stumbled and dropped Queen Victoria's coffin at her funeral. The resulting punishment was the Battery being banished from the UK for years. Killing Prince Andrew would certainly have been remembered, even if the Falklands War ended up being totally forgotten. Anyway, we were lucky: HRH was nowhere to be seen. We all cheered like kids at the bang, then ran like hell in case we were seen by the Officers. They were probably doing the same thing, though – and they did seem to end up with the best spoils of war. Mercedes Jeeps mysteriously seemed to find their way on-board UK-bound ships in the name of Captain So-and-So or Major Thingy. Yes, rank does have its privileges.

One afternoon Scouse and I were out for a stroll when we suddenly noticed a load of squaddies we didn't know cheering and waving to us rather enthusiastically. Being polite sorts, we waved back, all friendly-like and wondering why they were being so pally. They were shouting something, but we couldn't quite make it out.

It sounded like *'You're in my field,'* so we laughed and shouted back some abuse.

They just started waving and shouting all the more and then it suddenly clicked: You're in a *mine*field.

In a heartbeat, the colour drained from both of our faces and the joking stopped. We spent 15 minutes carefully retracing our steps, and were both shaking and close to tears by the time we got out. Minefields are still a problem on the islands today. The Argentineans laid them pretty indiscriminately and didn't bother keeping maps, which says something about the seriousness of their claim to the place: if you really thought you owned it, you'd be a bit more careful, surely? Worst of all, in some cases they laid 10Kg anti-tank mines and incorrectly set the pressure plates to anti-personnel. If you stepped on one of those you'd get a hell of a surprise, and several British soldiers were killed by mines in the aftermath of the war.

Once we'd recovered our composure, we saw another group of our lads kneeling down around a hole in the ground. Not wanting to miss out on anything we wandered over to them, though a little more carefully than before.

'What have you lot found?'

'Look at the state of this bastard.'

In the hole was what was left of an Argentine soldier. The head and arms were completely missing and all that remained was his torso and one leg. As we'd not fought infantry battles we hadn't seen many corpses, so it held a macabre fascination for us: we were like children happening upon a dead fox in the woods. Two of the soldiers had sticks and were prodding the remains, trying to prise open his rib cage. We were all giggling like adolescents as the two with the sticks started to flick bits of rotting flesh at each other. One of the lads ended the game by throwing a small Argie grenade into the hole. We scattered, running in all directions as a dull thud sounded behind us and sent mud and human remains into the air and all over us in a shower. The guys drunkenly howled like Red Indians, looking for more mischief.

This act was to haunt me to this day. It was a shameful thing to do, impossible to justify or even to explain, and I have asked the dead soldier for forgiveness for being part of it. In our defence, all I can say is that we weren't ourselves that day. We hadn't been ourselves for a while. The war had de-humanised us and we didn't give too much of a toss about anything. I suppose that fact that it bothers me now, over thirty years later, proves that I wasn't turning into an animal or some kind of automaton. Being drunk on vodka at the time was not a good idea either. One day two gunners were arguing at our accommodation, the old weather station, we were existing in, one of them threatened to kill the other one, we were all drinking alcohol again, which didn't really help with our severe diarrhoea, and our conduct with lethal weapons, I said something like, 'Go on then mouth', and gave one of them a loaded FN rifle, he grabbed the weapon, aimed it at the other lad, who went white and sobered up pretty quickly, luckily for all of us, he never pulled the trigger, Scouse Denmark bravely intervened and took the weapon of him, God knows what would have happened if he hadn't. The gunner holding the rifle on that day is still a serving senior rank member of the Royal Artillery, what a difference and few ounces of pressure on a trigger can make?

Our bodily functions were giving us serious grief after a week in Stanley. In fact, the wild shites went through the Battery like the Black Death. I remember legging it to the nearest bit of dirt, pulling down my combats and squirting diarrhoea like water everywhere, not sure whether to laugh hysterically or scream with the agony at the worst stomach cramps you can imagine. You never felt finished; no sooner had you got back to the lines when another stabbing pain would hit you you'd start off again, bent over, clutching your guts. I still suffer from IBS to this day.

It's not surprising, really. We had no proper washing facilities and there was filth and excrement everywhere. We were living like pigs. Eventually, the powers-that-be decided on an emergency evacuation onto a ferry, the *St Edmund*, to assist in the repatriation of POWs back to Argentina and give us some proper sanitation. I was really looking forward to that task: visions of hot showers, good scoff, beer and real beds dazzled my brain.

Paradise.

It was just as well, too. We were beginning to look like concentration camp victims with all the weight we had lost due to the sickness and diarrhoea.

We soon settled into our new environment and started to feel much happier with our lot. We put clean clothes on and got assigned duties, mainly guarding the prisoners. This was probably the best part of the war for the Argies. Most of them were just young conscripts and they had been treated appallingly by their superiors. Here they were being well-treated under the rules of the Geneva convention – four meals a day, tea breaks, medical attention, the lot, and they were lapping it up. We were stagging on, watching them smoke, play cards and generally have a good time on their way home courtesy of HM the Queen Cruise liners. Some of our lads struck up a friendship with one or two of them but it was too early for me. I still felt a lot of hatred, though not so much for the ordinary squaddies like us but for their Officers. They got preferential treatment: they were given the best accommodation, with the best food in their own mess. We kept winding them up by telling them we were taking them to Chile where they would be executed by our South American allies.

What really pissed me off was the fact that we had to wake them up in the morning with a cup of tea in bed. Apparently, this was Red Cross rules. We had our own little T Battery way of doing things. Taff had pinched a loud-hailer from somewhere, and every morning we would gently open their cabin doors, sneak inside, put the loud hailer next to their heads and then scream, 'Morning Argies!' as we prodded them with our rifles. 'Chile, Chile, next stop Chile, what a lovely morning to die.'

We'd then drag in the tea urn for ten seconds and then drag it out again before they had chance to get to it.

'Too slow, never mind.'

Well, they were Officers and we hated Officers, especially Argie ones.

When we were guarding the buckshee Argie squaddies we made sure they got their brews and fags OK. You could tell by their faces that they were genuinely grateful and, apart from one or two of the regular Army gung ho types with them, they didn't bear us any malice. They'd just been doing what they had been told to and they were glad the whole nightmare was all over. Mind you, we still had our fun with them from time to time. The majority of them were held in the car deck area, where they sat, well-behaved, row after row of black hair and dark-skinned faces. Apart from one. In the middle sat a lad with blonde hair and pale skin.

I pointed at him.

'Come here, mate.'

He looked up sheepishly.

'Yes, you. Come here.'

He stood up and timidly walked towards me, standing in front of me, head down and shaking. I don't know what he thought I was going to do. I certainly had no intention of hurting him. To break the ice I gave him a boiled sweet.

'Where are you from in Argentina?'

'I am not from Argentina. I am from Holland.'

'From Holland?'

He went on to tell me that his family had moved to Argentina as his father had got a job there. When the Malvinas were liberated he was forced into the Army. He didn't know anything about soldiering and had survived during the battles with the British by hiding himself under the corpses of his fellow soldiers. I gave him some more boiled sweets for his troubles and not wanting his fellow captors to be suspicious of him I took out a handful of sweets from my pocket and threw them into the pen. They scrapped like mad, a mass of tangled arms and legs just for a poxy boiled sweet. That was it: I'd invented a new sport, 'Argie wrestling'. Every time I was asked to guard them, I would bring a tin of boiled sweets to pass the time away.

Another luxury the POW's got was a shower. It was our job to take them and make sure they didn't stay in there all day due to the limited amount of water on board. Ninety nine per cent of them were great and did exactly as we told them, but there was the occasional smart alec. Most of them understood enough English to turn the water off and get out when we told them to.

I remember one prisoner who understood perfectly well but decided he wasn't ready to get out yet. He even had the neck to start singing; he must have been an Argie Paratrooper, I would think.

I shouted, 'Water off, out now!'

It wasn't fair on the other prisoners, who were waiting patiently – and we didn't have unlimited water.

He carried on soaping himself and singing away.

I put my hand in and turned the water off. He still had soap in his eyes and he just lost it, pushing me, rabbiting on in Spanish.

Have you ever tried to grab a soapy, naked prisoner in a shower? Believe me, it's not easy. But I managed to get my forearm under his chin and pull him out and as he turned away from me I put my boot up his arse for good measure. He went skidding down the corridor some distance due to the soap on him and the shiny floor and came to rest at the feet of two startled Red Cross representatives who had just turned the corner. Their surprise at being confronted by a naked Argie apparently body-surfing through the ship quickly changed to outrage at my treatment of the prisoner. Curtly, they asked my name, rank and number before heading off to report me to our Officer Commanding.

Later in the day, I was marched in to see GBH. He told me that the Red Cross had protested in the strongest terms at my treatment of a prisoner. He had assured them that the guilty soldier would be severely punished. I was then allowed to explain the reason for my actions. I related the story, explaining the waste of valuable water and the fact that there was a risk of discipline breaking down with the other POWs as this one laughed and took the piss.

GBH just said: 'Next time, make sure the Red Cross aren't about. Dismissed.'

I had marched in, thinking, big fine and extra duties, and marched out thinking, good old GBH.

Most of the Battery had planned to smuggle their stolen, illegal weapons aboard so they could take them back to Blighty. The BQMS had been clever, though. He'd slyly asked us to hand over the FNs and other kit 'for safekeeping'. Like soft lads, we all did as he asked, labelling our weapons carefully with our names and passing them into storage. We never saw them again and we were told after the conflict that they had been thrown into the sea on the journey back. I doubt it, somehow. I still had an Officer's Colt .45 stashed away, anyway.

We dropped off our batch of POW's at Montevideo, in Uruguay, and sailed back to the Falklands.

We spent another week back in Stanley, cleaning up again – they even sent us round the island picking up wool, of all things – and becoming increasingly fed up with our Senior Officers for not sending us home. One of our lads had a lucky escape when he found a booby trap of a grenade hidden in the wool. Our sister Battery, 9 (Plassey), had landed by now and had started deploying to our old positions. Although the war was over, Britain's attitude to defending the islands had changed and air defence was part of the new approach. Surely we could get going now?

(Incidentally, 9 Battery had spent the whole conflict, at sea in the exclusion zone, and had qualified for the same medal as us. It's no wonder that, after the war, some of our kills were claimed by 9 Battery in pubs around the UK. They were the blue-eyed boys of 12 Air Defence Regiment, something the CO proved when, back in the UK, he addressed T Battery. Most of his speech was about what a wonderful job 9 Battery were doing on the Islands, how they were under constant threat of a new Argie counter attack, and were in as much danger as we had been under during the war. That speech alone was probably responsible for half of T Battery leaving the Army.) But I am sure if 9 Battery, had to fight they would have done so with utmost bravery and professionalism.

A second month had now elapsed since the formal surrender of all Argentine forces on East and West Falkland on 14th June. I'd reached my 20th birthday on 11th July.

I was no longer a teenager, but that was the least of it. I felt like an old man.

HOMEWARD BOUND

Eventually, the news that we were all waiting for came through: in a day or so, we would be sailing to Ascension Island and then making the last stage of the journey home courtesy of the RAF.

Eagerly, we cleaned all of the Battery's equipment and vehicles and then loaded it aboard the *Norland*. As the ship set sail, there weren't too many of us standing on deck wistfully watching the Falkland Islands shrink away into the distance. The general feeling was, *Thank God we're out of here and on the way back to civilisation. Now let's get to the bar and get shit-faced.*

There was some serious boozing done on the journey and I was drunk from the moment I went on board. Alcohol is a depressant, they say, and after drinking vast quantities of the stuff I certainly did become depressed. I remember sitting at a table, surrounded by empty beer cans, ranting and raving like a gibbering idiot. Everyone else was in their own drunken world. I started crying, bawling like a baby. And nobody noticed. Through the tears streaming down my face, I could see the BSM and some NCOs staggering around like out-of-control dodgems. I felt like throwing up, so I went up on deck. It was late at night, and I leaned over the rail looking into the icy depths. I was overcome by this huge urge to jump into the sea and escape from this ship full of madmen. Would I have jumped? Probably not. Maybe. I don't know. Scouse had followed me on deck. He came up and leaned on the rail next to me and asked if I was alright.

I told him that I wanted to jump.

He laughed and said something like, 'Don't be a soft bastard.'

I grinned, the moment passed and we both staggered back to the bar for more beer, until unconsciousness overcame us. I really think I would have jumped if he hadn't showed up, and I don't think I ever thanked Scouse for that. Thanks mate.

When me and Scouse weren't pissed, we used to recce for goodies. One mission on the car deck brought us to a wooden crate hidden under some cam-nets. We prised the lid off to find it stuffed full of Yorkie bars and Arctic ration packs. After about three or four trips, we had removed a goodly portion of the swag to our cabin, where we stuffed our faces in secret over several days, enjoying the extra rations all the more because they were stolen. But 20 Yorkie bars a day takes its toll on you. I've not eaten one since the Falklands – I can't even look at one without thinking of that journey – and I've have to be close to starving to do so. I'd had a similar experience as a fourteen-year-old Army cadet. I was at a gala in the Lake District. Once we'd finished our demonstration of field craft and weapon drills to the public, we went for a look round. It was pretty obvious where the drinks tent was, but we were too young to be served. We were sat on the grass wishing we were eighteen when one of our mates signalled us to follow him. We leopard-crawled to the back of the beer tent and pulled up a flap. We each stuck our head inside to see what was there. Right in front of us were some crates of beer and some spirits. We decided to pinch a huge bottle of whisky and between four of us we drank it all that night. I was sick as a dog; head stuck in the toilet, shouting for my Mam, dad saying, 'Leave him alone, that'll teach him to drink.'

I promised I'd never drink again and while I broke that one, I've never been a big one for Scotch ever since.

There were ructions on the journey home, more than there'd been on the way out probably, with everyone letting their hair down and drinking far more.

We shared the ship with 4th Field RA and The Scots Guards; the latter were totally nuts, running up and down the ship's corridors all night, pissed out of their skulls, playing the bagpipes and fighting, usually with each other thank God. There had been the odd scrap between us but the best ruck I witnessed was when one of their Majors removed the crowns from his lapels and laid out a rather inebriated Jock Guard, to the whooping delight of everybody, including the lad's mates. That's something you don't see every day.

There was obviously a bit of tension between the Scots and the English and, by and large, we stayed out of their way. There were two reasons for this. Firstly, we were heavily outnumbered. Secondly, they were psychopaths. This did present me with a great piss-taking opportunity, though. Walking along a corridor one morning, I noticed a group of Scots Guards coming towards us. In one of life's odd coincidences, one of them was a mate of mine from Dalton-in-Furness. As I walked past, I casually said, 'Alright, Wilbour?' He looked around, saw me and couldn't believe I was on the same ship. We shook hands, had a chat and a laugh and I told him my cabin number; he said he'd be around that night for the craic. Then I doubled back to find the lads in my cabin. I told them I'd just had a massive barney with some wooden-tops (Guardsmen) and that they had said they'd be around later to kick my English head in, along with those of any other RA wankers who wanted to know. I was slagged off all day for being such a daft bastard and letting them know our cabin number.

The tension was pretty high as we sat there waiting for it all to kick off that evening. Looking around the room, the other boys looked like they were expecting a rematch of the Battle of Bannockburn.

About 8 o'clock, Wilbour knocked on our cabin door.

Taff says, 'Who the fuck's that?' in his hardest voice.

I told him to go and answer it, but he decided he'd rather not and invited me to go and answer it myself, *you pillock*.

I jumped off my bunk and opened the door to find a smiling Wilbour standing there. I slammed the door in his face and shouted, 'It's the Jock Guards, come on, give us a hand.' Then I opened it again and dragged a now-bemused Wilbour in. They all looked like scalded cats, expecting major mayhem and I couldn't help cracking up. They nearly killed me. I introduced everyone to Wilbour and we got pissed and smoked crushed-up aspirin. Why we smoked crushed-up aspirin I have absolutely no idea. It seemed like a good idea at the time but it does absolutely nothing for you. It doesn't even cure headaches. We spent a few hours reminiscing, me talking a bit about what T Battery had got up to, how a Rapier works, that sort of thing, and then we listened to Wilbour's war stories. He told us about the battle of Tumbledown, a savage hand-to-hand fire-fight which had played a major part in finally breaking the Argentinean resistance. He'd seen one of their Officers, Lieutenant Robert Lawrence, shot in the head by an enemy sniper. This man lost 40% of his brain matter in the shooting, but recovered well later and the episode was to be the basis for the BBC film *Tumbledown*. That kind of put our experiences into perspective.

We had a fair few evenings like that, chewing the fat, talking bollocks to each other and were getting on famously with the Jocks by the end. Too famously in once case: a Lance Bombardier was found in bed with one of the Scots lads. His excuse was that he had somehow got into the wrong bunk, and hadn't noticed the six-foot-three Guardsman in there. Well it was obviously a mistake anyone could make.

Things quietened down a bit after one of our lads, Chimp from 31 Delta, got in a fight over an illegal weapon and a lad called Fozzy stabbed him in the stomach with a bayonet – only just enough to break the skin, luckily. This prompted the senior ranks to call a parade (during which, ironically, a big scuffle broke out) and warn us that on arrival in the UK, each man would be thoroughly searched and their equipment put through a metal detector. Anyone found with illegal firearms would receive a seven year jail sentence and a dishonourable discharge. That night I went up on deck and threw my prized Colt .45 pistol into the sea. It was a wrench; I'd found it lying in the mud around Stanley, where its Argie officer owner had dropped it, and I really didn't want to let it go. But there didn't seem to be much choice and I'm sure there were other lads doing the same. The ironic thing was we weren't searched at customs after all; you could have driven a tank through if you wanted and the strong rumour doing the rounds at the time was that the officers had kept all *their* stash hidden behind the panels of the Rapiers.

We got off the boat at Ascension Island and spent a few hours soaking up the warm sunlight at the USAF's Wide Awake Airbase. It looked a hell of a lot better, after the Falklands, than it had on the way down. There was even a duty free shop on the airbase and I bought a large bottle of vodka before making my way to the aircraft. I'd assumed we would be flown home on some noisy old C130 Hercules but was pleasantly surprised to find we would be travelling by a comfortable – and much quicker – RAF VC10. I fully expected some officer to haul us off the plane after we'd boarded – 'Sorry chaps, been a bit of a mistake, this is for those elite fellows, the Marines… you're swimming home' – but somehow it never happened.

Everything was happening too fast. We were in pleasant surroundings being served hot food by gorgeous – or at least, female – RAF flight crew. The smell of perfume and the sight of real women at close range was hard to take after months of squaddies, sheep and shit, I can tell you.

We landed at Dakar in Africa to refuel. The local government were touchy about us being there and wouldn't allow us inside the terminal so we lounged around on the Tarmac in scorching heat while lots of bare-footed airport workers eyed us suspiciously. After about an hour we were back on board and in the air again. The African sun had drained me so, after a few gulps of neat vodka, I fell into a deep, intoxicated sleep, to be woken five hours or so later by the Captain's voice on the Tannoy informing us that we were entering British air space. A massive cheer erupted around the plane and I started craning my neck to catch a glimpse of land out of the window.

I was looking forward – as we all were – to a glorious homecoming.

An hour or so later, the aircraft landed and taxied to a halt.

We'd made it. We'd been to war and come home alive.

I had no idea what to expect when I left the plane. A mixture of alcohol and excitement made me, and many others, unsteady on our feet. We disembarked in order of rank, so I was one of the last to stagger down the stairway, to the stirring tunes of a military band and the waves and smiles of a small crowd of civvies, and a gaggle of press men. At the bottom of the stairs were several high ranking Officers. In my excitement, I nearly forgot to salute them and the drunken effort I did make wasn't exactly Trooping of the Colour standard.

I was engulfed in a sea of emotion as families embraced, hugging and kissing in an unashamed display of love and relief.

But amongst all these people, including the men I'd just fought with, I felt totally alone. Nobody from my family had come to meet me. I wasn't really all that bothered at the time; it's only as I write this, nearly 35 years later, with both my Mam and dad dead and gone, that I feel sad that I was alone on that day.

Sometimes I imagine the events in my mind, how I would have liked them to have been. My parents and my sister, my girlfriend and some of my civvie mates are stood on the runway, shouting to me and waving Union Jacks. Someone has a bottle of champagne and is shaking it up like a Formula One winner, there's ticker tape flying around and one of the Officers comes over and shakes my hand. I wander over, and hug and kiss each one of them in turn, a few tears in my eyes. I shake hands with my father and he says he's proud of me. I have a long, lingering kiss with Carole, and we all go home together to celebrate.

Sadly, I don't live in Hollywood: I stood there, alone, in my combats and 58 webbing, unsure as to what to do next. Nobody was giving me any orders. I was confused. Suddenly, an arm appeared on my shoulder. It was the Lady Mayoress of Lincoln, offering to be my 'mother' for the day. It felt a bit odd, but I had my photo taken with her by the local newspaper and I would like to thank that lady, if she's still alive. She was the ambassador of the entire British people for me with her simple, kind gesture.

Eventually, the Army restored some order with Officers and NCOs striding around and shouting at us Gunners. It didn't take long – I'd been back on English soil for ten minutes and they had me loading the Battery's kit onto Bedford trucks. After we'd got the kit aboard we were loaded up ourselves onto white Army buses and driven back to our barracks at Kirton-in-Lindsey.

As a reward for winning the war, the Army let us have the weekend off. We were supposed to be back at work for first parade, 0800 hrs, Monday morning. Home was too far so I decided to stay in Kirton. My plan was to see Carole and somehow get her back to the block for a leg over. I knew I'd have the room to myself as the other lads had gone home. I was so keen to see her, I went straight up to her house in my combats, still clutching my half empty bottle of vodka as soon as they let us fall out at Kirton.

I arrived at her house and rang the bell.

She came to the door, looking rather shocked to see me. I guess I was in a bit of a state.

We went to a local pub together. I began drinking heavily, and swearing like... well, like a trooper.

Carole told me people were looking. I said I didn't give a fuck and asked her to come back to the block with me.

She refused, saying she was scared of the other soldiers though, looking back, I was obviously the problem.

I told her that we'd be alone, but she wouldn't change her mind.

My new post-war personality emerged: I called her a slag, and a cow, and asked her which civvie had been shagging her while I was in the Falklands.

She ran out of the pub in tears.

I woke up the next morning, on the floor in the block, covered in puke and blood. I must have busted my nose somehow, or had it bust for me, but I couldn't remember it happening. Slowly, through the fog of the booze and the pounding headache, I remembered what had happened with Carole. I went to phone her to apologise; she told me that she didn't want to see me again, and that I had been acting like a total stranger.

Then she put the phone down on me and I never saw her again. Carole was the first casualty in my own, new war. It was a war that – at the time – I didn't even know I was fighting.

SURROUNDED AND ALONE

WE spent the next week in the barracks sorting out the kit and cleaning the place up. It was typical of the Army; it's rules for the sake of bloody rules at times. Surely they could have waited till we came back from our (much-delayed) three-week block-leave?

Still, leave came around eventually and I had about £1,000 worth of beer tokens to spend. I headed north with every intention of spending most of the time in a drunken blur.

I remember walking into my house for the first time since I'd been away. I had been looking forward to this moment for months – imagining my folks' uncontrollable joy at the return of the hero – but once again my expectations were somewhat wide of the mark. My dad was sat in his usual chair watching the TV. He looked at me like I'd just been to the shop for a packet of fags, said hello and we shook hands before he switched channels. My Mam was obviously happy to see her son home safe again but she wasn't exactly demonstrative about it: she was a quiet and unassuming woman, just glad that lighting all those candles in the church had paid off.

It was all a bit of an anti-climax, and from there it descended into farce, but I was home.

To give them their due, the neighbours across the street had hung bunting out and there was even a party organised for me at the Cavendish Arms in town. But I just felt so miserable, even at my own party. Everyone was really friendly, but they all asked the same questions.

The lads all asked: 'Did you kill anyone?'

The girls all asked: 'What was it like?'

The only reply I could give them to the first question was, 'I don't know.'

The only reply I could give to the second – the same one I give to this day – was, 'It was freezing cold, and there were no trees.'

The only people I could talk to about it all in any depth were other soldiers and veterans of other conflicts. I remember half-way through my party I snuck out without anyone noticing and walked up the road to a little pub. I spent the rest of the night getting quietly pissed in the corner.

The neighbours must have thought I was a right ignorant bastard, but I just wasn't comfortable in the spotlight.

Things didn't improve much with the folks. I suppose they were from a different, less expressive generation, but then other lads had great welcomes from their parents. Maybe it was me? It certainly didn't help matters when I went totally berserk with my family a week or so into the leave. We had a row about something irrelevant and I smashed up the house and stormed out. That night, I dug a trench in the garden and slept in there, wearing my combat gear. I was on permanent stag, chasing local drunks down the street if they had the cheek to sit on my wall. It was obviously very odd behaviour – though I didn't realise it at the time – and I slid further and further out of control.

The worst thing was that I just couldn't sleep properly. I'd never had trouble getting my head down before, but now I'd wake up, often in a cold sweat, at 2am or 3am, and find myself replaying the events of the attack on the *Galahad* over and over again in my head. My dreams were all bad ones and I started getting very down about it.

I went out looking for trouble, and managed to get myself barred from most of the pubs in Dalton inside a week. Things came to a bit of a head after another screaming row at home: my dad called the police and they said that they would arrest me if I didn't quieten down.

None of this was really like me, or like the old me, anyway. I'd always been a fairly placid lad. I'd changed, but no-one, including me, seemed to understand how or why. I managed to stay out of trouble for the last few days but, by the end of the three weeks, I just wanted to get back to camp, to mix with the lads, my mates who understood what had happened down there in the south Atlantic. I felt like things would be back to normal there.

I picked up a paper on the train on the way back down south and was shocked to read about the death of Paul Stimpson, a Gunner from T Battery and a really good lad. He had been killed riding his motorbike from Kirton to Scunthorpe. A lorry had been parked up on a bad bend and Paul had ridden straight into the back of it. What a bloody tragedy, all the more so soon after he had survived the war.

It must have been dreadful for his parents: one moment he's home and safe, the next he's dead. A terrible accident. (In memory of his Paul, his father painted a scene of San Carlos. It took pride of place in the T Battery offices.)

For some reason, maybe it was my two kills; I was picked to represent the battery marching through London in the victory parade after I got back. It was the proudest moment of my life, wearing my South Atlantic medal for the first time. I'll remember forever the huge crowds cheering us on as we passed up to the Guild Hall for a slap up meal with the Iron lady herself, Maggie Thatcher. The one disappointment for me was that the Queen couldn't make it because she was away in Canada. Normally, she would have taken the salute but the Iron Lady took it instead. Well, it was her war, her victory and her country at the time.

I was really proud to be a soldier that day, we all were, and I wouldn't have changed that for anything. Take me back three or four months, though; the crowds watching the victory parade would have seen 32 Alpha, huddled together in the dark like frightened lambs, praying the Canberra night-bomber above our heads didn't destroy us and our missiles.

After those heady few hours, it was back to the mundane, peacetime duties of soldiering: guard duties, cook-house fatigues, sweeping leaves. All bull and even more bullshit. The Falklands was well and truly history, and wasn't life totally boring again.

My nightmares continued, and a few of the lads told me I'd woken them up by shouting and thrashing around in my sleep. I was drinking more and more, and found myself provoking fights with other soldiers, which was something I'd never done before. More than once I had to be dragged off someone who'd looked at me in a funny way; a few of the lads thought I was going a bit nutty, and others gave me a wide berth. I just thought they were the weird ones.

I didn't make a conscious, considered decision to leave the Army. It just happened one day. I was stood on top of a one-ton Land Rover, about to hand a cam-net down to Bob.

I shouted out, 'Bob, where do you want this?'

Bob shouted back, 'Over here Mack' and I lobbed it his way.

I hadn't noticed, but a young Lieutenant straight from the factory (Sandhurst Military Academy) had entered the garage; he was a fresh-faced strip of a lad, bristling with pride and keen to stamp his new-found authority on the place. He looked me up and down and proceeded to give me a bollocking about addressing a senior rank by his first name. A Rapier detachment always worked as a small, close-knit unit and during the war we'd all been on first-name terms. I understand the need for discipline and rules, of course, though I still question whether this sort of humiliating dressing-down serves any useful purpose. I was wound pretty tight and I just didn't need this little idiot quoting The Queen's regulations at me. In fact, I was filled with an almost irresistible urge to punch him in the face. I didn't want this rubbish any more. I felt different now, I felt I'd proved myself in a war. 32 Alpha were my mates, Bob included. We had a bond. Something snapped in my head. *Fuck you,* I thought. *I'm getting out of this shit.* Something that I'd never properly experienced as an adult – civilian life – suddenly had an appeal.

Some of the Battery had already signed off and in that sudden moment of temper, I followed them, storming off to the pen-pushers in the Battery office to jack it in.

You had to give the Army a year's notice, which gives the Army one year to make your life a misery, but I stuck it out and finally left in June 1983. During the first four weeks of freedom, I was still officially a soldier. This is for the benefit of the Army, so you don't take the opportunity to hang around and settle a few old scores (such as with jumped-up little lieutenants who can't tell you what to do any more).

It maybe wasn't the best decision I ever made. Britain in the early 1980s was not the best place to be looking for work, especially if you were an ex-boy soldier with a short fuse. I got a couple of jobs – I worked part of the time as a security guard at the shipyard and also got taken on as a process worker in the Cellophane factory, thanks to my dad.

I was free of all the rules and pointless discipline and the yes sir, no sir bullshit that was all I'd known for the last few years. But the grass is always greener, isn't it?

I wasn't the same guy who'd left Dalton any more: yes, the Army was a pain in the arse in many ways but it had its plus points. Chief among those was that you didn't have to think for yourself too much. Your food and accommodation was taken care of and there were always plenty of lads to go on the piss with in the evenings. After a while, back living with my parents and clocking on each day, I slowly began to realise that I'd just swapped one lot of bosses for another. I still had to obey rules – it was just that now they were my mom's and work's.

It wasn't quite the nirvana I'd been hoping for. I was still drinking very heavily and seemed constantly to be fighting the flu and, though my military discipline meant I never missed work, it wasn't long before I started half-regretting getting out. I'd find myself idly imagining the boys out getting slaughtered and having the craic together and wondering why the hell I'd allowed a little bollocking from an insignificant 12-year-old officer to wind me up quite so much.

I decided that the best compromise, if I wanted to be a soldier and stay a civvie, would be to become a mercenary. I had been reading *Soldier of Fortune* magazine for a few years – all soldiers do – and I put an advert in offering my services. I received replies from other Brits who wanted to be mercenaries as well, as well as a load of hate mail from Parachute Regiment members – the usual crap-hat insults. I only received one serious reply, from a Texan Vietnam veteran who was recruiting for an operation in Africa. I put it to one side but then received more letters from this Yank. In the end, I wrote back saying that I was interested. The operation was scheduled for June 1986 and a meeting was to be arranged for the recruitment of European personnel in London. I'd booked a holiday to Rhodes with my civvie mate, Russ. We had the usual two week lad's holiday, and I ended up with alcoholic poisoning. After staggering off the flight home at Manchester, I bought a *Daily Mirror* and was surprised and somewhat horrified to find my ugly mug plastered all over it above an article about my mercenary advert in *SOF*. It had the cheek to say that I was still a serving soldier but the damage was done; I decided to bin the idea of being a mercenary after all. It later emerged that I'd made the right choice. Rumour had it there was an operation involving British mercenaries whose mission was to make cross-border raids from South Africa into Mozambique to destroy oil refineries. Unfortunately for them, the Mozambique Army was being trained at the time by a BATT (British Army Training Team) who ambushed the dogs of war, killing many of those involved.

The one thing I had going for me was Julie – she was the daughter of a family friend, and we'd started going out in the summer of 1985.

Even that wasn't enough to tie me down, though. Scouse had left around the same time as me and, after going through the same feeling of rootlessness and boredom, he had joined up again. He rang me up from Germany one day, sounding like a little kid with a new toy and telling me how brilliant the Regiment was. They had tracked Rapier now, he said – it was just like driving a tank…I had to get back in.

I told him he wouldn't see me back in the Army, no way, bollocks, what kind of mug did he take me for?

The next day I went to the Army Careers Office in town to see if I could re-enlist and I found myself back in 12 Regt in April 1986.

Surprisingly, nothing was mentioned about the article in the *Daily Mirror*. I avoided having to do basic training again, even though I'd been out for nearly three years, and re-joined T Battery to become a tracked Rapier missile operator.

It *was* like driving a tank, too.

Of course, human nature being what it is, I soon tired again of the endless fatigues, with the odd exercise thrown in. I found myself back in Dortmund at Napier barracks, and the best part of that was the B1 road to Ostende and the ferry home. So I volunteered for service in Northern Ireland with 74 Battery 32 Heavy Regiment Royal Artillery.

The good thing about Northern Ireland training was that 32 Regiment were also in Dortmund, so we could live in our accommodation and commute to work each day. There were four of us from T Battery – me, and three other lads, Big Taff May, Coddy and Ashtray Anderson. Ashtray was the son of a surgeon from Carlisle and spoke with a very posh accent. One day, he was smoking a fag. Instead of flicking his ash on the floor like 99.99% of squaddies would, he leaned over and said – in an accent more than a little reminiscent of Dirk Bogarde – 'Pass the ashtray.' Job done, he was 'Ashtray' forever more.

Initially, training involved patrolling around Moore Barracks getting shot at by other squaddies pretending they were terrorists.

Then we went on rural training at Haltern Ranges, where I got bitten half to death by midges and my hands and face swelled up like balloons and Taff made a name for himself by putting salt in the tea urn.

Next was a unit search training course, probably the most enjoyable course I did in the Army. Our instructor was a Sergeant from 9 Para Royal Engineers and he was as cool as a cucumber. The course did exactly what it said on the tin: it taught you to search things. However, we had to be trained for any eventuality, prepared for the unexpected. To ram this point home, they used lots of little tricks. One involved your chair. As you sat down, it exploded; not exactly a thousand pounds of Semtex, but enough to make you wake up, that's for sure. Others were more painful. One day they wired our steel urinals up to a 9-volt battery. As soon as you started an electric current shot back up the stream or urine and into your tenderest parts. At the end of that day we all had extremely full bladders.

The atmosphere on course was relaxed, as opposed to the usual 'get your fucking feet together' Army style. Due to the nature of the work involved, a patient and methodical approach was needed. In the early seventies, a British Army search had consisted of a sledgehammer taking the front door off at 0600 hrs and a gang of squaddies trashing the place. But the fact of the matter was not that every Catholic house was a PIRA bomb factory and a squaddie acting like a Chelsea fan at West Ham could quickly turn a respectable family into a Sinn Fein propaganda coup. So we were trained to search in a more civilised manner, accompanied by the RUC (the Royal Ulster Constabulary, the disbanded forerunners of today's Police Service of Northern Ireland) and a search warrant.

With our bag of tools, we looked more like a plumbers than squaddies. One team of two would search upstairs; one team of two searched the ground floor. One thing was drilled into us if we ever found anything suspicious: 'Don't touch!' This was for a number of obvious reasons. It could go bang, in a nasty way, but we could also disturb evidence. In the unlikely event that we found an M16 assault rifle under the bed, picked it up and it didn't go bang, the residents would insist that they had never seen it before now that our Brit fingerprints were all over it.

One training search in Sennelager was memorable. Our team was tasked with searching a mock-up house on the ranges complete with squaddies acting as hacked-off Catholics. They were really looking forward to giving us grief, but they didn't plan on the reaction of Taff. We were the upstairs crew, and Coddy and Ashtray took downstairs. We were met on the doorstep by an 'irate family', complete with mother and sister courtesy of the WRAC. Going through the motions, we explained what we were doing, produced our search warrant and NISR (Northern Ireland Search Report) and tried to enter. They responded with an Academy Award-winning performance, screaming and pushing us back out of the door. It was like a red rag to a bull for Taff: he ran straight through them and set off up the stairs, me in his wake. The foolish 'male occupant' stood halfway up the stairs, blocking our progress and screaming 'Fuck off out of my house.' This upset Taff's gentle south Wales's nature and he responded by literally picking him up and throwing him head-first down the stairs like a sack of spuds. Well, they wanted realism. The guy was knocked spark out, smashing his nose on the door handle at the bottom and landing in a heap of blood and snot. We'd made it to the top and started searching. I did the toilet and Taff did the large bedroom. He'd gone mad by this point, though, and I found him bouncing up and down on the bed with a pair of knickers he'd found in a drawer on his head. What we didn't realise was that the large mirror on the wall was two-way and that behind it, observing our 'search', was the instructor. The exercise was quickly brought to a halt and an ambulance was called for a pretend Irishman.

At the end of our training, we were severely tested on all aspects of our task at a place known as Tin City. This was designed to be the closest thing you could get to Northern Ireland without being there, a mock-up town with houses, streets, shops and a very hostile 'civilian population'. Every incident we responded to was recorded on film and sometimes played back to everyone in the cinema, which often resulted in some poor squaddie going the colour of an RMP beret as he watched himself take up a firing position next to an exploding car or dustbin. It was important to take it all very seriously – no dancing around with knickers on your head here – it could be hard to do so. One day, I stopped a car full of my mates from T Battery, who were part of the 'civ pop' (the civilian population). Each member of the civ pop was given a new identity and date of birth so a lad I knew was about 20 was posing as a 75-year-old. The final, farcical nail in that day's coffin came when one of the terrorists handed me my mail from camp. Oh, the realism of it all.

One thing which could be guaranteed at Tin City was that every day there would be an incident of some kind to deal with. As a result, by the time we actually got to Northern Ireland we were expecting it to resemble the Wild West, with a terrorist lurking round every corner waiting to shoot at us as soon as we stepped off the plane. It wasn't like that, of course, and there was a danger that once we'd calmed down we'd go too far the other way and get lulled into a false sense of security. To avoid that, the NITAT (Northern Ireland Training Advisory Team) showed us photographs of dead British soldiers. One picture that particularly stuck in my mind was a photo of two lads who had gone over the wall in Belfast to spend the night with a pair of old boilers from Sandy Row. This was a loyalist part of the city so the squaddies must have thought that they would be safe. Once the two were naked and vulnerable, the door was booted in and two masked gunmen from PIRA interrogated them before shooting them at point blank range between the eyes. Those shots certainly sent the required message from my brain to my knob. They also showed us pictures of dead terrorists, though, and that cheered us up no end.

Northern Ireland training completed, the British Army decided 74 Battery were ready to be prison guard force at HMP Maze.

NORTHERN IRELAND

When I was a schoolboy Army cadet in the mid-1970s, Northern Ireland was on the news nearly every night, kept there by a seemingly constant diet of bombings, shootings and riots. As kids, we pretended we were in Belfast as we hard-targeted around cars and bus stops on our way home after drill nights, clutching pretend weapons in the shape of vaguely rifle-shaped bits of wood. Once I joined up, there was always a lot of talk about the Paddies from the old sweats that had done tours of NI. So even when I left the Army after the Falklands, I – foolishly – never felt like a complete soldier because I'd never been over the water. Wanting to have a crack at that was one of the reasons I had re-enlisted.

We flew to RAF Aldergrove in Belfast and were transported to HMP Maze in the back of soft-canvas Bedford wagons with an RMP Land Rover at the front and another at the back for our protection. Perhaps they planned to keep PIRA at bay with their rule books? To say I didn't feel very safe in this mode of transport would be an understatement. More than once, and not for the last time, I found myself questioning my own sanity.

The Maze or 'Long Kesh' the former RAF station as it used to be known on the outskirts of Lisburn was a top security prison, the most secure in Europe, full of paramilitary murderers from both sides – the kind of boys who would shoot you as quick as pick their nose. Security was tight and you were always aware that you were a target yourself. We took over from a cavalry regiment who had written the usual 'stag on' graffiti everywhere and I soon found myself up one of the towers sited along the perimeter walls. You were in there for four hours at a time and all I can say is that if you had kept livestock in such conditions you would have been prosecuted. A Land Rover would drop me off at the assigned tower where a Junior NCO was supposed to frisk you to ensure you weren't carrying any contraband – girlie mags, alcohol, Walkmans etc – stashed in your respirator case. He would usually just ask me, though, and I would lie through my teeth and proceed to the ladder. At the top of the ladder there would be a trap door, which gave access to the watchtower, you own personal, urine-soaked airborne cell. At first, I used to wrinkle my nose in disgust; those cavalry bastards… why did they have to piss in there? Then I needed a piss myself, and found there was no toilet. There was an impressive array of weaponry. In addition to my personal weapon, there was an LMG with about 300 rounds, a baton gun or FRG (Federal Riot Gun) with plastic bullets, smoke grenades, a Very pistol, a night sight and a radio (military type). There were also binos, a log book and a small electric heater that sometimes gave off a modicum of heat until you were forced to turn it off due to the stink of the sweat and other bodily fluids left there by the previous thousand occupants.

The first few stags, I did everything by the book. I didn't want to be responsible for the second breakout from the Maze, the first, on 25th September 1983, 38 IRA prisoners escaped. Some were caught a few miles from the Maze waiting at a bus stop. Mind you, a lot got away, some of them to the USA where even if they were found they were safe. Back then, the Americans wouldn't dream of extraditing known, convicted IRA men back to the UK; that would have upset the 'Irish-American' vote. If you want a parallel, imagine the mastermind behind the 9/11 Twin Towers outrage being found in Britain and our government refusing to hand them over. I know 9/11 was bigger than anything PIRA achieved, but it wasn't for the want of trying.)

So, I did my duty: prompt radio checks, filling out the log book, observing my arcs of fire and just occasionally flicking through my illegal copy of *Penthouse*. By days two and three, though, I was taking more interest in the reader's wives pages in *Fiesta* than the cows chewing the cud in the fields on one side of the wire and the prisoners playing netball on the other.

And so it went on, every boring day the same as the last. We were lucky not to get excitement of the wrong kind, however. The last duty before knocking off after a night on stag was to leave the Maze in a mobile and check the perimeter for anything suspicious. We would have been on duty for the last twelve hours, would be utterly shagged and all we'd really have on our minds was climbing into our pits. I can't speak for other units, but while 32 were at the prison this patrol was done at the same time every day, bang on 7am. Looking back, I'm surprised – and relieved – that the IRA didn't have a crack at a very soft target.

It didn't do my morale much good when I spent time on stag on the main gate with a Prison Officer who had just earned twice in a week what I would take home in a month. Mind you, they deserved it. They had to live there.

After a while, any glamour the place might have had in my mind had worn off. I'd stand there thinking, *What an idiot. I can't believe I volunteered for this shit. They say never volunteer for anything – the NIGs still get caught out by 'Who can ride a motorbike?' – And they're right.*

But I thought, *Fuck it, let's go for a death wish* and volunteered to spend a fortnight at North Howard Street Mill, a West Belfast Army outpost, with 2nd Battalion Light Infantry. In other words, actually doing the job that the taxpayer had spent all that money training me to do, patrolling the streets. I know it sounds mad but I'd have done anything to get out of those mind-numbing, wrist-aching, soul-destroying towers. I was going stir crazy and blind.

I was driven into Belfast in what was known as a 'Q car'. Named after the Navy's World War Two 'Q ships', which were anti-submarine vessels disguised as trawlers and the like, these were military vehicles made to look like they belonged to local civvies and supposed to blend into the urban environment. This one was an old Ford Transit van with the rear windows blacked out. We might as well have had a neon sign on the roof flashing 'British soldiers'. But it was just good to get out of that horrible jail and, as I peered through the little pinholes in the window, I saw a city going about its business, apparently oblivious to the current troubles.

We reached the Mill safely and I was shown my accommodation, a small room with about ten bunk beds crammed inside. All the other beds were made up, apart from one in the corner. I assumed this must be mine. There were a couple of infantry lads in the room and they made me feel at home straight away, cracking jokes in their Geordie accents. I asked them if the empty bed was mine. They said it was, but as I put my kit on the bed they went very quiet. I didn't think much of this as I unpacked, made up the bed and waited for orders. I found out later the reason for their change of mood. The empty bed had belonged to one of their mates, a lad who had been shot a couple of nights earlier. I had actually heard about the shooting on my civvie radio up in my tower. The casualty was doing 'top cover' at the time; this was done by two soldiers, standing up in an open hatch in a Land Rover and facing in opposite directions to sweep the streets with their weapons, hopefully providing a full 360 degrees of all-round defence. You are looking for anyone trying to endanger the mobile with an improvised explosive device or even a common or garden petrol bomb. Of course, you're pretty exposed up there to any cowboy who fancies taking a pot shot at you and this soldier had been hit by a 5.56mm round. This had almost certainly been fired from an American-made M16 Armalite rifle. Unlike the British Army SLR 7.62mm round of the day, which spun as it cut straight through the air, an M16 round tumbles towards its target, making it much more devastating on impact. The round had hit the lad under his armpit, missing his INIBA (Individual Northern Ireland Body Armour) vest, with its armoured Kevlar plates in the front and back designed to protect the wearer's vital organs. Once inside, it had bounced around off a few ribs before travelling down his torso and, amazingly, exiting behind his knee. He didn't realise that he'd been hit at first and it was only when he felt the dampness of the blood that the pain hit him and he passed out. Apparently, the locals soon realised that a Brit had been hit and began cheering and throwing bricks and the usual supply of petrol bombs. An ambulance was called but they stopped it by blocking the street; the bastards obviously wanted him to bleed to death. His light infantry mates had soon cleared them away with baton rounds, however, and the soldier was rushed away to the Royal Victoria Hospital, where he made a full recovery, luckily.

And I had his pit space.

Just to make me feel better, the lads told me that the last time they had had a Gunner seconded to them, oddly enough from 32 Regiment RA, he had been killed by a Provo with an M60 machine gun.

I remember my first patrol, a mobile in a 1950s Saracen armoured car. It may have been old, but it was a mean-looking bastard and offered better protection than the soft-skinned Land Rovers that some of the guys used in the early days of Iraq and Afghanistan, which is a shocking indictment.

As we were putting our magazines on our SLRs in the loading bay, I noticed the vehicle backfiring, with all sorts of loud bangs going off and black smoke everywhere. I assumed they'd find us a replacement – after all, what would we do if it gave up the ghost somewhere down the Falls Road? – but then the army doesn't really work like that.

'Mount Up!' shouted the brick commander, and we got in. It was the first time I'd ever been in a Saracen and I was looking forward to it until I got inside. I've rarely been more claustrophobic – you had to watch you didn't put someone's eye out with your rifle. The back door was slammed shut, and we heard the vehicle commander check his radio comms with Zero.

He had a quick chat with the RCT (Royal Corps Of Transport) driver, showing him the map references, and we started to backfire, lurch and smoke our way out into West Belfast.

I was the only gunner aboard, in a brick of infantry lads, and they didn't seem too happy to see me. They kept shooting looks at me, obviously wondering what this loon with the blue beret was doing there. I did wonder myself; the infantry beret was khaki, which meant I stuck out a bit. As I sat there, I imagined an IRA sniper spotting us.

'Hmmm… which one shall I slot? Begorrah… I know, the one with the blue beret. He must be an officer or something.'

We'd been travelling a few minutes when the brick commander shouted 'Top cover up!'

There was hesitation, as the soldiers all looked at each other; no-one seemed to want to leave the relative safety of the armour and they were all clearly hoping some other mug would do it. Then they all turned to me. You didn't need to be a mind reader to work out what they were thinking.

If he's stupid enough to volunteer for Northern Ireland, he must be stupid enough to volunteer for top cover?

The commander shouted again, louder this time. 'I said Top cover up!'

Still there was no movement, which really wound him up. This time he literally screamed. 'Harris! Get your fucking head through that fucking hatch!'

The squaddie shouted back that he couldn't, because he didn't have his gloves with him. Seriously – that was the best he could do. I had mine on so I leaned forward.

'I'll go up,' I said.

'No, you fucking won't,' screamed the commander. 'Harris, you get up there or I'll fucking shoot you myself!'

Reluctantly, and gingerly, the infantryman climbed up through the hatch.

Just then, the driver stopped for a red light and, as the vehicle came to a halt the engine died. On the Springfield Road, which was right in the heart of the Republican area of Belfast. Not good. It wasn't as though we could call the RAC, and every second we sat there gave the Boyos time to spot us and get themselves organised.

The lights changed and behind us a line of irate morning commuters, oblivious to our fire-power, started beeping their horns and yelling for us to get going. All eyes in the Sarry Can widened slightly, and we gripped our weapons a little tighter. We were one big, metal IRA target and going nowhere fast.

Up front, the RCT driver was frantically trying to restart the engine. I heard him tell the commander he was worried about flooding it, and I also heard the commander's terse reply that it might be flooded with lead and RPGs in a minute. It seemed like a lifetime, but it was probably only 30 seconds or so before it roared back into life and we trundled off, leaving a trail of oily, sooty smoke and irritable Irishmen behind us.

I looked around at the other soldiers, all lost in their own thoughts. It was too loud to talk properly, so I sat there and tried to focus on the patrol. Then I heard what I assumed was a brick hitting the side of the vehicle – a sharp bang, like a whip cracking in the air.

Even though he wasn't supposed to, the top cover soldier slid back down sharpish, a lot quicker than he'd gone up. Onward we drove and the unlucky squaddie was ordered back up top with threats of a punch.

As he did so I heard the brick commander radio his contact report back to Zero: we'd just been shot at.

The lads in the back didn't even raise their eyebrows. *Maybe it was like this every day?*

Urban patrolling was actually a dodle compared to the rural work, stuck out in the 'cuds', where you would sometimes walk for miles, getting ripped to pieces by gorse and constantly wet-through in the rain. You couldn't just nip into the local RUC nick for a brew, either, because chances were a reception party would be waiting for you when you came out.

In built-up areas, by contrast, most of the time it was just a stroll in the sun, eyeing up the women. Despite this, I was always on edge. I had one embarrassing moment in Ballymurphy, West Belfast, when a lad of about five threw a stone which hit me smack bang on the back of the head, much to the huge amusement of the infantrymen. He probably got an extra bag of sweets for that one from his mother. It was quite upsetting to see how the parents seemed to want their kids to get caught up in it all, to perpetuate the hatred, though I suppose to them we were an occupying Army, invading their country. I guess we wouldn't much have liked seeing German squaddies walking up and down Dalton.

VCPs (Vehicle check points) were a crucial way of interrupting the terrorists' freedom to transport weapons and explosives around the province and, maybe, even catching one or two of the main local PIRA or criminal players.

They were also deadly dull: 99.9% of the people you stopped were law-abiding citizens going about their business – most of whom didn't even know where their bonnet release catch was, let along how to strip and reassemble an Armalite.

Some days it was so quiet that you to guard against being lulled in to a false sense of security. I recall one VCP near the main M1 motorway that flows between Dublin and Belfast. We were all standing around a Ford Cortina going, 'That thing's your engine, love... what's that there, you say? Well, that's where you put the oil' to the nice young lass who owned it, as one of the lads went through her boot. I was next to an RUC man who was counting down the minutes until his next large glass of Bushmills, it wasn't raining for a change and the VCP was flowing nicely. A brand new red Astra pulled up to one side and I watched one of our lads approach it.

So far, so run-of-the-mill.

Next thing, all hell broke loose, with the squaddie physically dragging the driver from the car and pinning him to the Tarmac, a boot on his head and the barrel of his SLR pushed into his face.

We all dropped to one knee and fanned out, taking up firing positions and wondering what the hell was going on. The soldier leaned into the car and lifted out a holdall full of gym kit... and a nice, chunky-looking .45 automatic.

It turned out – amazingly – that the driver was an RUC officer. For some reason, he'd not bothered to mention that to the soldier and he'd also omitted to mention the pistol in his bag. Very stupid: he could have been shot if the lad had been really jumpy. I'm sure the IRA would have loved that.

On another occasion, we were on mobile patrol out in the cuds and we had set up a 'snap VCP' – a quick, 15 minute check-point which is up and down before the terrorists have time to organise themselves and come and have a pop at you. We'd usually pick a spot just around a bend so that the vehicles would be on us almost as soon as they were into the straight and would have no time to stop or turn back before they were within our cordon. We stopped an old blue Transit van with four guys in the front. The driver wound his window down, all stony-faced. That didn't necessarily mean he was a bad lad – many ordinary folks got fed up with our VCPs holding them up and restricting their movement, and I didn't blame them – but it was an interesting sign.

I started chatting to him, while the RUC element ran a number plate check.

'Where've you been then, lads?' I asked.

'Rabbiting,' he said.

A couple of them were dressed in t-shirts, which was funny gear for rabbiting; I was in my combats, and still chilly.

'Oh, yeah? I used to do a bit of that myself when I was a lad. Caught any?'

'No.'

Sometimes you could have the craic, a bit of leg-pulling, but there wasn't much banter with these four; either they hadn't kissed the blarney stone, or they really didn't like Brits.

The RUC guy wandered over. The number plate was dodgy, so we had the four of them out of the van. Right on cue it started to rain, and they stood there getting soaked to the skin. Again, this was odd: Joe Public would have been whingeing by now, but these boys never said a dickey bird.

We gave them and the van a thorough search and found nothing; we reported this to the RUC man with us.

He wasn't happy. 'Keep the bastards in the pissing rain and search them and the van again,' he said.

I thought this was going a bit far; I was search-trained and there was nothing in there, but the copper was obviously enjoying his power. I went through the motions again and shouted 'Clear!'

I was getting annoyed myself by now, never mind the four blokes; this was pointless, and the longer we were there the more chance there was of the wrong people noticing us. The other soldiers were getting edgy, too, and everyone was on a higher state of alert as the minutes ticked by.

The RUC officer didn't seem to care too much. He came over and looked them all in the eyes. Then he turned to me. 'Have you searched inside their shoes?'

Before I could even say 'No' they had taken their shoes off and were standing on the road in wet socks. The RUC guy went and got himself a hot brew and spent five minutes drinking it, leaning against the Land Rover talking to our brick commander. By the end of this charade, the four stood there in the rain for over 40 minutes and didn't once complain. They obviously wanted to avoid arrest at all costs.

Eventually, he let them go and they drove slowly away with the copper waving at them sarcastically.

I'm not saying they were whiter than white: they were obviously known, or at least travelling in a vehicle which was known to have been used by Republicans, but I couldn't help thinking that this sort of thing was only going to perpetuate the whole situation. And if by chance they *were* entirely innocent, that RUC man had just created four new Nationalists that was for sure.

He wasn't the only one with a counter-productive manner about him. One afternoon we stopped a minibus full of handicapped kids. As they got off the bus, a stupid, heartless squaddie started taking the piss out of them. We were soon surrounded by a group of furious mums, foaming at the mouth and, quite fairly, slagging us off. They were spitting in our faces, pushing us and grabbing at our weapons: things were rapidly getting out of hand. I could see their point, to be honest – I could quite happily have shot the idiot myself, and done them all a favour. As things threatened to get out of hand, we were ordered to move. As we set off up the street, followed by a barrage of insults and house bricks, an Army chopper appeared, hovering just above us, and suddenly the street was empty. This was not a good sign: the natives were always quick to make themselves scarce if a PIRA gunman was in the offing. Luckily, nothing happened and the CO tried to defuse the situation by apologising profusely to the locals.

There were always happy days to be had patrolling the Divis Flats, a run-down, graffiti-splattered hornets' nest of republicans which stank of stale piss and old hatred – a bit like our towers at the Maze, really, Soldiers had been seriously injured by people throwing tellies and fridges out of top storey windows. Imagine that on your headstone: 'Here lies Gunner McNally, killed in action in Northern Ireland by a flying fridge freezer.'

It wasn't just household white goods: used nappies and sanitary towels and bags full or urine and excrement were regularly lobbed down on us. They were lovely people, they really were.

All too soon, my two weeks at the Mill was done. I'd really enjoyed it, surprisingly, doing some real soldiering, but now it was back to stagging on in the towers.

After a month or so, we'd all got into a routine and would play Trivial Pursuit. One man would read the questions through the tower intercom system and we'd all battle it out for a piece of plastic pie. This, and playing tapes down the line, helped pass the time. We all had a chance of being DJ for the night; I would play songs like *Alternative Ulster* and *Suspect Device* by Stiff Little Fingers, just to cheer everyone up, alongside stuff by The Clash and the Sex Pistols. Tough shit if they didn't like punk. I'd have to listen to their disco crap tomorrow.

Yes, we were thoroughly professional; as I'm sure the lads had thought they were on the night of that big escape.

At about 0100hrs one morning, I was on stag when I heard singing and shouting on the road. It was some Prison Officers, ex-squaddies, coming out of a staff disco full of Guinness. They started shouting up at my tower. 'Stag on you tosser,' and 'I'm off home now to shag the missus, who's shagging yours?'

Not known for their wit, those boys.

Shortly after that, I escaped the towers once more. I put my name down, along with many others, for duty on board a Royal Navy minesweeper which was being tasked with the searching of vessels at sea for arms and other contraband. To many lads, for some reason, this seemed a better option than being shot at or showered with shit on the streets of sunny Belfast. Given my extensive experience of, and family background in, seafaring it was no surprise when I volunteered. I hurriedly packed up my kit and set off by Q car for Moscow Barracks. Who would have thought that volunteering for Northern Ireland would see you at sea with the senior service?

The boat was small and wooden, with a crew of large matelots. There's a belief, fondly held throughout the Army, that the entire Navy is composed of poofs. If these lads were poofs, I wasn't teasing them about it because they were poofs who looked like Arnold Schwarzenegger. Because we wore camouflage combats, the Navy amusingly liked to call us 'trees', or the more usual 'pongos'. I pointed out that they were only jealous because their bosses made them wear bell-bottoms.

My first night on board, we were still in dock. Some of the crew got changed into civvies and asked if I was coming into the city centre for a pizza. I declined their invitation and spent the night at the NAAFI bar at Moscow. Even though they were sailors, they were still Crown Forces and, therefore, the enemy to the Nationalists. Their hair might have been a bit longer, and one or two had beards, but they dressed the same, off-duty, as us, in the instantly-recognisable second uniform of jeans, trainers and tee-shirts. Their mainland accents wouldn't have helped much, either.

After we set sail, I was assigned to the night search duties. I'd be woken in my bunk by a Tannoy message from the Captain, jump into my all-in-one rubber suit, and cold sea water in the bottom of my wellies just to wake me up, and find myself skimming across the Irish Sea about three minutes later, hanging onto the sides of the rubber intercept boat for dear life. Most times it would be a false alarm, a civilian yacht which had strayed off course or something similar. We would still board and search, of course. One night, we had received information that a vessel was transporting illegal arms and explosives for loyalist terror groups. Part of me thought, *What are we bothering with them for? They're doing us a favour.* The reality was, though, that the majority of loyalist killings were mindless sectarian jobs, so the weapons being smuggled in could be used to murder an innocent Catholic for no other reason than his religion. It was extremely rare, as far as I'm aware, for loyalist terrorists to kill genuine IRA members.

We'd been tracking the suspect vessel for several hours and the Captain decided the time had come to intercept and search. As it would be a night operation my search team would be carrying it out. Orders were completed. I was to be the only tree. I wondered whether the Navy realised I was in the Royal Artillery, and not the SAS, but it was too late to raise that now. With my trusty tool bag and 9mm Browning automatic pistol holstered, off I went. As we sped across the Irish Sea in pitch darkness, I clung on to the sides of the boat with cold wet fingers, idly wondering what chance a rubber boat full of matelots and one slightly queasy Gunner had against a heavily-armed ship full of psychopathic terrorists who didn't much fancy a twenty-year stretch in the Maze.

How the fuck did I get into this? I asked myself, once again.

You volunteered, stupid.

Appearing out of the sea spray, I could just make out a light on top of a mast. As we got nearer, I could figure out the shape of a yacht. The actual boarding was over within seconds. The Royal Navy Officer produced a loud-hailer and announced boldly that we were Her Majesty's Forces and that they should be prepared to be boarded. So far, so good. Nobody was shooting.

I was first on board, where I was immediately confronted by a panicking Frenchman shouting 'Pirates! Pirates!' in a hysterical voice.

Our Officer calmed him down with a few French phrases and explained that we weren't actually, pirates and what we were there for. We then carried out our standard search of the boat and found nothing but wet, stripey tee-shirts, black berets, loaves of French bread and a couple of strings of onions.

And as things turned out, we'd done the two-man crew a favour: they had a problem with their radar and weren't exactly sure where they were. In fact, they were dangerously close to the rocky Irish coast so we contacted the Coast Guard and arranged safe passage for them into port so they could find their bearings again and get some garlic and cheese down their necks in safety.

As we bounced our way across the sea back to our mother ship I thought thank Christ it had turned out like it did. At the de-brief, intelligence was still adamant that the real target vessel was still out there somewhere. We just had to keep looking. Well, that was someone else's job now. Mine was done for the night. I handed my tools and pistol in and got back in my bunk to dream of Blighty.

And you know what, sometimes dreams do come true.

We were to have 24-hours' shore leave, and docked at Bangor, North Wales. Some of the crew from that area went home.

I considered going home myself to see Julie, but the long distance put me off so I stayed in Bangor on the piss.

I couldn't believe my luck.

A tour of Northern Ireland and I wind up back in the UK on leave.

I knew Taff wouldn't believe it either so I sent him a post card.

He still didn't believe me and said I'd rang someone in the UK and got them to send it for me.

Even after being at sea for one week, when I got ashore I felt land sick again. It reminded me of when I first got off the boat in the Falklands.

Perhaps I should have joined the Navy after all. I can't remember much about Bangor apart from a heavy beer drinking session.

I know I rang Julie up from a pay phone in a cubicle inside a hotel, and that we talked so long I had to use my pint pot as a piss pot. When my money ran out, I gave her my number and she rang me back and we talked for another two hours. I'd have hated to have had to pay her Mam and dad's phone bill.

Twenty-four hours gone in a flash.

All the crew got back on board and off we went again looking for the bad guys.

We never found any but it was good work and I enjoyed it. One day, in the middle of the sea in the middle of October, the mad bastard matelots dropped anchor and decided to go for a swim. I thought I'd give that a miss and locked myself in the heads, as the Navy were most insistent and were looking for a tree to strip off and throw in.

But all too soon my adventures on the high seas were over. I waved farewell to my bell-bottomed friends at Moscow Docks and caught another cunningly-disguised Q car back to the nick.

Our team was being sent to Portadown to work with 9 Ulster Defence Regiment. They were a funny bunch of lads, I found. There was a fair bit of animosity between them and us – it was as if they resented us being on their patch. This was a strange attitude, since we were a major factor in stopping the IRA from killing them and kneecapping their families. Some of them had big chips on their shoulders and a lot of attitude. I remember standing at the bar one night when a UDR soldier sidled over and pretended to be sociable. It was just an excuse to tell me how the UDR were God's gift to Ulster. It ended up in one of those pointless arguments fuelled by beer – he reckoned the UDR could do the job better than the regular British Army and I disagreed. It was like a game of ping-pong and eventually I realised I'd get more sense out of Gerry Adams and pissed off with the rest of our team. It came as no surprise when they were disbanded, especially if this guy was anything to go by. In the UDR's defence, he was English. Probably ex Devon & Dorsets, or something. There was a lot of this sort of thing but to be honest I didn't really care: the food was good and there was a disco on camp every Saturday night.

The discos were good fun but a combination of drunken soldiers, regimental rivalry and toss-pots like the one above can be a rather potent mixture, and there was always the potential for it to kick off in a big way. One night I though World War III was about to break out. It had passed relatively peacefully and a few of our lads had bagged off with female UDR members who generally looked like Bernie Winters with his face kicked in. I just got thoroughly gutted, for a change. The custom in loyalist Northern Ireland is to stand to attention at the end of the night, when the National Anthem is played. Fair one – when in Rome, and all that. I stood to a rather wobbly attention with everybody else but I couldn't help noticing everyone staring in our direction, and not in a nice, friendly way. I had to check I hadn't worn a Sinn Fein t-shirt by accident. No. What was it? I turned round and, to my horror, there was Taff, slumped in a chair with a pint in his hand, ostentatiously failing to stand. Halfway through the anthem, several UDR members headed over towards us. One of them asked why my pal wasn't stood up and showing his respect for the Queen.

'Go and ask him,' I said.

So he approached Taff, and asked him.

'Who the fuck are you talking to?' said Taff. He was a big, solid lad, and he stood up in his own time, blacking out the light with his huge frame. He pointed to the lurid red dragon on his t-shirt. 'I'm fucking Welsh. That's not my fucking anthem and don't you tell me to fucking stand up, boyo, unless you want a smack in the face.'

Hmmm. Six of us, against a battalion – not very good odds.

A fighting withdrawal was on the cards.

Taff wasn't in the mood to withdraw, though. 'Come on then, I'll take you all on,' he said.

Thanks, Taff, we're dog meat.

After a few tense minutes of eyeing each other up, the UDR decided to let us off and we all continued to turn beer into piss.

We spent the rest of our time at Portadown without major incident. The only bit of fun occurred in the centre of town when the republicans were holding a rally with the usual end-of-night bonfires in the park. As a group of teenagers passed our mobile, giving us the usual torrent of anti-British abuse, I decided to wind a particular girl up by being nice to her.

'Youse can fuck off back to your Brit slum, you bastards,' she spat.

'You're a lovely-looking girl,' I replied, leaning out of the Land Rover. 'I don't suppose there's any chance of you going on a date with me?'

Her jaw dropped open and you could see the cogs in her tiny mind working overtime. Her brain clearly couldn't handle this approach.

'We could go to the pictures, or for a nice walk?' I said. 'Maybe I could come home and meet your Mam and dad?'

She froze in bewilderment, and then re-engaged her hate gear.

'You what? You Briddish scumbag!'

'Shame,' I said a pleasant smile still on my face. 'And I suppose a shag's out of the question?'

Howls of outrage and a small rainstorm of bricks and bottles headed our way, as the RUC Officer sat in the back of the Rover shook his head and tut-tutted at me.

November arrived, and we had completed our tour without injury or loss of life. Some Jock Regiment was taking over from us so we left a little graffiti around the place informing them that we'd be making a point of going up north to knock their wives off when we got home, and then made our way back to RAF Aldergrove in the same Bedfords we'd come in for the flight back to Germany.

I had achieved what I had dreamed about as a young Army cadet: a tour of Ulster. I was also to receive my second and last medal of my colour service.

Like most things, Ireland wasn't what I'd expected but it was better than sweeping leaves and painting Land Rovers. Though at least sweeping leaves and painting

Land Rovers was still an option – I still had my arms and legs, unlike many unlucky soldiers before me.

Anyway… Been there, done that, not going back.

But we were met back in Germany by the CO of 32 Heavy Regiment who promptly dropped a bombshell by informing 74 Battery that the whole of 32 Regiment were going back to Northern Ireland in the New Year. A least I was OK because I was 12 Regiment. Wrong. On return to my unit, I discovered 12 Regiment was going to Northern Ireland in the New Year as well.

Around that time, the MOD mandarins had decided the infantry were being rotated between tours too often and it was about time that non-infantry Regiments did their bit. Rightly so in my opinion. There were far too many over-weight soldiers in 12 Regiment that were happy passing their time away in the MT or handing out blankets in the BQMS. The only problem was, I'd done my share. Going back might be pushing my luck, I thought, especially with some of the idiot NCOs in our mob.

My mother had recently been diagnosed with Alzheimer's disease and my father was finding it increasingly difficult to have to look after her. This, and the thought of going back over the water to be spat at, nappied and possibly bombed, led to me deciding to sign off again. I applied for rear party; four months of that prior to getting out would give me ample time to sort out a job in civvie street.

Before T Battery started Ireland training, there was a trip to the Hebrides to live fire Rapier. This was a bit surprising. I knew the IRA were well in with the Yanks but I didn't realise they were supplying them with fighter jets. I was told by my Troop Commander that even though I was getting out I would have a missile allocated to me and off I set.

When I got to the Hebs, I wasn't allowed anywhere near the missiles and instead spent the whole two weeks being ordered about by fat, bearded, Hebridian women who would have looked at home in the movie *Deliverance*. The bastards had lied to me. But why? I was just a low-life Gunner. I had to do whatever they had ordered me to do. I can only conclude that they took pleasure in messing me about. Nothing new in that, that's what I joined up for. As my bloated white hands scrubbed my hundredth dixie I realised I had made the right decision to leave this time.

The Army's argument was it would be pointless to let me fire as opposed to a Gunner who had just joined up. This ignored the fact that once I was back in Civvie Street I would likely be put on reserve service and if the Soviet Bloc proverbial hit the fan it was quite possible I could have found myself behind the controls of a Rapier again. This negative attitude to soldiers who have signed off destroys any hope of them changing their minds. You were just a 10-a-penny tin can to be kicked around by everyone above your rank, and in my case that amounted to a lot of tin can kickers.

On arrival back in BAOR, I was stiffed again by a dose of T Battery double standards. The same senior Officer who had decided I wasn't worth a missile was now sending me to Northern Ireland after all, as T Battery were short-handed.

So I started Ireland training all over again from day one, even sitting there 'learning' the rules of engagement and basic patrolling skills. The team Commander was a REME Sergeant who acted like Frank Sinatra: everything had to be done his way. During one day's training, I offered some advice to him when we were alone. His response was, he didn't give a toss if I'd done a hundred tours of Northern Ireland, he was in charge.

That was it. I decided then and there I wasn't going anywhere with a bloke who obviously had a problem with man-management and would be a liability over the water. I patrolled past my accommodation window, where Scouse was stood in civvies, brew in hand, laughing his head off, and hatched my plot to be placed on rear party come what may.

Plan A. I asked for a Troop Commander's interview and ended up in the BSM's office. My story was that my father, who travelled regularly to Dublin, was worried about certain people finding out his son was a British soldier and had asked me not to go again. This tickled the BSM, Mickey Finn, no end; he laughed and told me how his parents were Irish, too, and it was just one of those things. I was going to Ireland, end of chat. March out.

Plan B. I asked for an interview with the Padre, and told him the same story. This time, though, I added the part about my mother's illness. The Padre, having the rank of Major, went to see our BC on my behalf.

End result – my name on rear party.

And they say you can't beat the system.

I wished T Battery luck as I waved them good-bye and passed the time away before I returned to civvie street. It wasn't a bad few weeks. The Sergeant in charge of us was a right soft touch and you could get away with murder.

Once out in the Province, a member of T Battery did something unbelievably low. The Battery hadn't been in Omagh long when PIRA bombers ambushed a convoy of Army coaches full of young infantry lads on their way back to England. T Battery was first on the scene of carnage and death – I remember watching them on the TV and spotting some of my mates in the footage. The lads told me later that after the bodies had been removed from the wreckage, a soldier went from coach to coach looting the belongings of the dead. Over the years in Germany, thousands of pounds-worth of personal possessions had mysteriously gone missing from our accommodation. It must have been the same guy. In my opinion, he should have been put up against the wall and shot. There was another bastard in T Battery who constantly stole from the lads in the block. He was a pad (married personnel), and his favourite trick was to ask someone if he could leave his bag in their room when he was on BONCO (Battery Orderly Non-Commissioned Officer duty). Later on, he would 'inadvertently' leave his bag locked in the victim's room. He would then ask to borrow the lad's keys to get his bag, and all the money and goodies he could steal. Eventually, we all worked out what he was up to, but we couldn't prove anything. There was a lot that went on in T Battery, from Junior NCO up to Senior NCO level that the Officers turned a blind eye to. One Gunner even had his medals stolen in 1982 and I am happy to report that this year I helped him get them back. It's a shame, but that incident of looting is one of my last memories of T Battery; it was an honour to have known the rest of those T Battery lads – fantastic, loyal soldiers who wrote a piece of their Regiment's history in the Falklands.

A NEW LIFE

Scouse and I stuck our names down for a re-settlement course. The only real benefit to this was that we got back to England early. Re-settlement courses were a half-hearted attempt by the Army to train you for a civvie job inside two weeks. Whatever course you did, the qualifications weren't worth the paper they were written on. Who was an employer going to take on? A bloke who's learnt how to weld in two weeks at Catterick Barracks, or a guy who has served his time?

When we got to Catterick, the whole place was under five feet of north Yorkshire snow and it was absolutely freezing. The accommodation was an old Nissan hut, with a fire in the middle that you had to make yourself. We decided there and then that this wasn't for us. The course started Monday morning. I think it was diesel fitting, though it might have been flower arranging for all I can recall. The personnel present consisted of elderly soldiers who were crapping themselves at the prospect of civvie street and believed everything anyone in green told them – including a load of old bull about their 'excellent' prospects of a job after discharge. After queuing up in a snow drift for a lukewarm breakfast served by cooks who looked as though they had fought in the Crimea, we went to another icy cold Nissan hut for an exam on what we knew about our chosen subject.

I scored about 5%.

After our sheets were marked, the instructor read us the obligatory riot act. He started with, 'If anyone on this course doesn't want to continue, say so now, and we won't be wasting each other's time.'

Expecting no response, he began the lesson. When he eventually looked up, he saw me and Scouse sat there with our arms in the air.

We were sent to RHQ, another, larger wooden hut, where we were issued with a travel warrant by a rather diminutive RSM with a very high-pitched voice. He ordered us to make our way to Woolwich.

What happened at Darlington station was spontaneous and mad. Scouse got on a train to Liverpool and I went home to Barrow. I'll always remember the journey because there was no heating on the rickety old train and my legs were soaked through from my feet up to my knees. Next morning, I woke up in my own bed in

Dalton, officially AWOL. If you've never been in the Army, this might not sound that big a deal; after all, lots of people call in sick on a Monday morning, or just jack their jobs in and never go back. It's not like that in the services: they own you. You can't just walk away, and if you try you end up in Army prison. Despite this, I was strangely unconcerned. It was probably the fact that I had only about a month to do and I assumed they wouldn't mind.

Then it hit me.

I was bloody AWOL.

Shit.

I had to think fast.

The phone rang and my dad shouted me down. It was Scouse. He told me the RSM of Woolwich had just rung him and ordered him to get his arse down there pronto. Clutching at straws, I rang Woolwich and spoke to a Battery Captain, explaining that I had left the course because my mother was ill and that I was shortly leaving the Army early on compassionate grounds to look after her. He sounded suspicious, and told me he would ring me back in half an hour – obviously, he was checking out my story. But when he finally called back, to my relief and utter astonishment, he told me that I could stay at home. They would write to me when I had to hand my ID card in but I was, effectively, a free man.

Poor old Scouse didn't have a similar excuse so he dragged himself down to Woolwich as per orders and got his arse beasted by the RSM and stuck on guard duty for the remainder of his service. Well, you win some and you lose some. Scouse had got the better of me on more than one occasion, but I had the last laugh.

On 12th December 1988, I reported to Woolwich to hand in my ID card, and officially became a civilian. Ironically, Scouse was on guard duty; he didn't look too pleased to see me as I strolled by, a grin on my face and a spring in my step.

My regular Army service had definitely ended this time, although for many years to come I would still consider myself a soldier, in mind anyway.

Back out in the big wide world again, I felt very alone.

Being in the military is very easy in some ways. Everything is organised for you – food, living accommodation, what to do and when to do it, a herd to follow and monthly pay cheques to take with you on your way.

Now I had to think for myself. The first step was looking for employment. I managed to get a job with Securicor, picking up about eighty pounds a week. I actually didn't mind the work but I couldn't get by on that wage so I kept my eyes peeled for something better; six months later I spotted an ad for a job packing soap powder on an assembly line. A hundred quid a week wasn't much better, but I took it. The lad I stood next to on my first day said, 'Every time I turn around, there's someone else on the conveyor belt.'

I wondered why but I soon found out. It was one of the worst jobs I've ever had: twelve-hour shifts, days and nights, stood in front of a conveyor belt, unfolding cardboard boxes and loading them with more boxes full of soap. Right in front of me was a clock, and it was impossible not to look at it every five minutes. If I needed to go to the toilet, I had to put my hand up like a schoolboy and ask a supervisor. It was totally soul-destroying, mental torture, but it was a job and I stuck it for a couple of months.

I got out when, thanks to a strange twist of fate, I ended up getting my old job back at the Cellophane factory. While I was still in the Army, Scouse and I had written off for numerous jobs. In July 1989, he rang me to tell me that he had an interview at Cellophane. He got the train from Liverpool and I offered to meet him and drive him to the factory. As I knew my way around, the security guard let me show him to the personnel office. I sat in the waiting room and when Scouse went in for his interview I nodded in recognition at the personnel officer. I decided to go back to the car to wait, but on my way out the security guard told me that I was wanted back down at personnel. The end result was we both ended up getting jobs there. This was more like it: two hundred and thirty quid a week and my fingers, cracked and sore from constantly packing soap powder, could now heal up. That night, I gleefully told the soapies where they could stick their job.

In the end, Scouse never came to Cellophane – he injured his knee and couldn't make it over to start – but I was soon back in my old routine and happier with it, too. There were clouds on the horizon, though.

I met a good friend at the factory which would end up having fatal consequences in the years to come.

One morning, as I sat at the kitchen table with a cup of tea and a bacon sarnie before heading off to work, my dad told me he'd heard me screaming and shouting in my sleep. He was worried about me: I'd also gone back to sleeping in the garden, in a trench in my combats, and was permanently aggressive and angry. More than once, I'd chased lads down the road because they were sitting on the wall or making a row outside the house. It wasn't normal behaviour, but I shrugged it off, swilled down my tea and left for the day.

The bad dreams I'd been having since soon after the Falklands had ended were getting worse. I hadn't thought too much of them at the time – they were just nightmares. The odd one stood out: one night in Northern Ireland I dreamed I was being strangled, and spat all over Taff who was in the bunk below me. I was lucky he didn't put me into a permanent coma.

Maybe I should have asked to see the medics, though even if I had I don't think they would have listened. But it's all academic. I didn't. Partly, I didn't realise I had serious problems. Partly, it's just not the sort of thing serving soldiers like to talk about. You don't want to show any weaknesses because it can be a merciless environment, although I suppose I could have stood up to the piss-taking – it wasn't like I was a coward, or somebody who was trying to work his ticket out. I'd volunteered for an operational tour of duty in Northern Ireland, after all, though some would say that was the proof that I was crazy.

Maybe the Army should have picked up those early signs, but then it's very difficult to spot irrational behaviour in soldiers because they are always getting in fights, behaving aggressively and generally acting oddly.

Anyway, I had just blotted the nightmares out with heavy drinking and got on with life. I'd hoped they would go away in time, particularly after I left the service, but that wasn't happening.

As I headed to the factory, I pushed it all to the back of my mind.

This was something I was able to do, back then. On an even keel, earning a reasonable wage, with a steady girlfriend to keep me on the straight and narrow and living back home among my old friends and family, I was coping.

The work at Cellophane was a really positive factor, too: we worked as a small team of seven, which reminded me of soldiering in the Falklands or Ireland. There was good banter and camaraderie between us and the future looked OK. The job lasted for over two years.

Then one day – early in the December of 1991 – the suits in London made us all redundant and closed the factory down.

On the last night we all brought in beer and had a party. I was very sad at saying good-bye to my mates. We all said we'd keep in touch, but apart from one lad I never see any of them now.

I think I would have continued to cope OK if the factory hadn't closed down. Without that regular work and the feeling of security it brought, I began to disintegrate.

I felt really low, that I was a failure, even though it wasn't my fault the place had shut. I had just bought a house and was planning to marry Julie and start a family. This looked a long way off, now. My mind was full of negative thoughts and they started getting stronger and stronger.

As I sank lower and lower, the old Falklands nightmares really started in earnest, taking a frightening grip on me.

I couldn't sleep properly, and the odd snatches I got were plagued with strange dreams of death and horror – Argentinean planes flown by dead men, and the body of the enemy soldier we'd abused in Stanley, come half-back to life and looking at me accusingly. I thought a lot about the *Sir Galahad*, and would find myself in tears, wondering why the fucking Rapier hadn't fired, feeling a mountain of guilt on my shoulders for all those deaths and the awful injuries of many of the survivors.

I was only out of work for a week or two. Just before Christmas, I got an interview for a security job, took my Army references with me and tried to give a good impression. One of the interviewers was an ex-RMP, it went well and I got the job. It was good money, too, though I soon discovered the reason why. The average bloke wouldn't suffer the conditions we had to work under for anything less.

We were contracted to work at a local factory where they made a variety of products. In the old days, they had

had three guys manning their gatehouse but cost-cutting meant it was left to one man now and quite often that was me. After the first couple of days, I didn't want to go back. It was just impossible to do the job correctly on my own. Two telephones were constantly ringing – one internal, one external – and I grew to hate the pat little greeting you were made to give: 'Good morning, thank you for calling… how may I help you?'

While you're stuck on the phone dealing with someone upstairs, or giving some trucker directions from the motorway, visitors would enter the gatehouse and expect to be dealt with straight away.

Meanwhile, every wagon – hundreds a day – had to be booked in and booked out; you were required physically to check a seal on the back doors of the outgoing vehicles. Contractors coming on site had to be booked in and the insides of their vehicles checked, too.

Eventually, you had a line of lorries like something out of *Convoy* waiting to come in, engines revving, air brakes going off and horns sounding, another line waiting to get out and 15 or 20 assorted people milling around in the tiny gatehouse asking stupid questions and getting in your way. It was bedlam, a chaotic, nightmarish farce. One thing I had learned as a soldier was to have pride in my job; that was impossible here. Actual security was virtually non-existent and I tried to make this point to the management but I got nowhere. It was all about money; proper security costs pound notes, and lots of them, and they didn't want to hear that. Opinions were dangerous things, and voicing one saw you classed as a trouble-maker. Your name would end up in the supervisor's little black book, which meant you were on your way out.

I would get home at 1900hrs, head throbbing, eat my tea then have to iron a clean white shirt for the morning as I didn't trust Julie with an iron. We'd end up having a blazing row, I'd crawl to bed, fall into a coma and have several night terrors before getting up at 0500hrs and doing it all again, bleary-eyed and utterly knackered. After a few weeks of this, I couldn't cope with work. I hated it. I would fantasise about answering the phone: 'Good morning and fuck off!' before walking out at the busiest time of day, giving all the wagons the V-sign and heading to the nearest pub to get slaughtered. But I didn't have the guts to turn my fantasy into reality like always I soldiered on.

Security work always attracts ex-squaddies, and having people to talk to about my Falklands experiences helped keep me from sliding into total insanity. I'd spend meal breaks chatting with a lad called Taff, who was actually English but had been named Maldwyn by his Welsh dad. Taff was ex-Army Catering Corps and had served in Northern Ireland during Operation Motorman in the early seventies, in the mad, bad old days when IRA gunmen would stand openly in the street and have cowboy-style shoot-outs with the security forces. Another lad who I got along with well was a guy called Dave. He was an ex-infantry soldier and someone who would go on to play quite a significant part in my life.

Although I had quickly realised that it was impossible to do the job properly, I had to turn up and go through the motions. Julie and I were getting married in the November of 1993, so I just had to hack it; it wasn't just about me anymore. If it had have been, I would probably have been in Bosnia, or the French Foreign Legion, or anywhere else but that bloody factory.

We got married and honeymooned in Florida. We enjoyed Disney World, saw all the other sights and visited my auntie, who lived out there, and generally had a nice couple of weeks. But my head was nowhere near right. I was edgy and tense the whole time, though I tried not to show it, and starting to get paranoid. It was, I think, a combination of drinking, sleep deprivation – every night now I would wake up, sweating, caught in a night terror or dreaming about the *Sir Galahad* – and depression. Our hotel was in a fairly rough area, off the beaten tourist track, and several people had been murdered within a five minute drive of the place in the recent past. Gradually, I began to expect trouble: everyone who looked my way, that guy on his mobile phone, the gang of youths across the street, the kid who just dodged round that corner… they were all out to rob us and shoot us. It was as if I was back in Ireland, but this time I was unarmed.

The feelings of being threatened grew until I became convinced I was going to be shot, that it wasn't 'if' but 'when'. One day, I slipped away from the hotel and bought myself a second-hand Colt automatic pistol from a backstreet gun shop. It was a heavy, reassuring weapon

STILL WATCHING MEN BURN

that would stop a man in his tracks, well a real one would, but this one was a replica, just as well really. When we left, I disabled the handgun and tossed it in a river.

Obviously, these weren't the actions of a normal man, enjoying a relaxing honeymoon with his new wife but, at the time, it all seemed normal to me.

During our time in Florida, Julie started throwing up fairly regularly. I thought she had caught some sort of bug but women *know*, somehow. She bought a pregnancy test kit, and... Bingo! Sitting outside our hotel in 80°f sunshine, we had suddenly, and dramatically, become a family.

It was a nice surprise – we'd not really been trying for kids, but we soon came round to the idea, though Dave spoilt things a bit when he rang my hotel room from work in England to tell me that I'd been put on a new shift with a couple of blokes I didn't much like. It was obvious – to me – that they were trying to winkle me out of the place.

They didn't have to worry.

Dave was going to get rid of both of us for them.

Back home, my nightmares were coming thick and fast now, with a stressful job and hardly any sleep combining and feeding off each other in a vicious circle. It didn't help that I was drinking heavily – seven or eight pints a night, with spirits chasers – and that I was worrying myself sick about providing for a new baby.

One night, I woke up to find myself loudly screaming at Julie in the middle of a crazy nightmare. I was mortified, and she was terrified, more that I might hurt the baby than anything. A few days after that, Julie developed anaemia with the pregnancy and had to go into hospital, which left me on my own at home.

I found myself rattling around the house with time on my hands which, in my deteriorating mental state was a bad situation in which to be. My shift pattern had been changed and I was on my days off at the same time as Dave. So one night – January 6, 1994, as it happens – I went round to his house with a pack of beer, a bottle of Southern Comfort and a couple of violent gangster and War films. When I got there, his wife and two kids went to bed and we settled down for a quiet evening of Hollywood blood and gore.

We sat there, getting steadily more and more pissed and revelling in the bloodshed and aggression, when Dave suddenly told me about a local petty thief and low life who he was convinced had stolen one of his mountain bikes and scratched his new car. A detective in Barrow CID had apparently tipped him the wink that they knew this guy was responsible, they just couldn't prove it.

At this point, celluloid fantasy and Lake District reality became blurred in a sort of haze of adrenalin, hatred and booze.

Dave was ranting about how he wanted to deal with the guy and I went along with him, full of bravado and making mad suggestions of my own. 'The bastard's got no respect,' I said.

Dave got more and more wound up by the second, and then he disappeared upstairs.

He returned moments later, grinning like a Cheshire cat, and holding something wrapped up in a cam-scarf. He unfolded it and proudly displayed a sawn-off shotgun and several rounds of ammo. Cradling it like a father with a new baby, he told me he'd lent it to another guy earlier in the year. The guy had been threatened and wanted protection; unfortunately, when they came and started kicking in his door, the gun wouldn't work. It looked pretty serviceable to me – the idiot had probably forgotten to load it.

This was a view Dave shared.

He grabbed a combat jacket, picked up an S10 respirator (to be found lying in a corner in most homes, surely) and looked at me with a wicked glint in his eye.

'Come on,' he said, breaking it and slotting in two orange 12 bore cartridges. 'I'll show you the bloody thing works!'

As it happened, I was dressed in Para smock, black woolly hat, jeans, and boots and Northern Ireland gloves. You can take the man out of the Army, but you can't take the Army out of the man, not completely, anyway. Well, at least I was wearing the right gear for an op like this. But I declined his offer and decided to go home to my pregnant wife instead. Stupidly I had left my fingerprints on the gun and even more stupidly for Dave he went on to fire it that night through the window of his targets house.
Later that night I was followed home and arrested by an armed response unit.

I protested my innocence, which did me a lot of good; my 'dabs' were all over the gun, we were both jointly charged with possession of a sawn off shotgun with intent to endanger life. I was certainly guilty of being stupid.

I was in a state of shock, especially when a grinning copper advised me that the maximum sentence I could get for this was life.

I should have stayed in tonight, I thought.

I had started reading a book called *The Feathermen* – an everyday tale of everyday contract killers, psychopathic mercenaries and black ops – at the poolside in Florida. I finished reading it in a dirty, smelly, cold police cell in Barrow.

Oddly, in a mix of emotions, I felt some relief that my security job was finished. In fact, it seemed as though my working career was probably finished for good.

As for myself, there are only two things I can say in my own defence.

The first is that firearms and soldiers go together. It seemed to me totally natural for Dave to be stood there in his living room holding a loaded weapon and looking murderously left and right, whereas I can see that it might not seem at all natural from a civilian point of view. Dave was also a trained British army sniper. Once again I know what Dave did was wrong, but in mitigation, Dave had also served in Northern Ireland, he was on top cover in an army Landover and some youths had thrown a paving slab off a bridge hitting Dave on the head, smashing his helmet in two pieces and seriously injuring him, he was lucky not to have been killed, mitigating circumstances? I don't suppose the police officer that gave Dave the information in the first place realized what the consequences of telling him were, but he obviously should have known better, in such a position of authority.

The weather station incident in the Falklands and the incident at Dave's had parallels, both involved, alcohol and firearms, with a good measure of stupidity and bravado thrown in, one was in a theatre of War, one was in a living room in peace time, with women and children asleep upstairs, those involved were soldiers, or in the latter case ex-soldiers, men that had a lethal firearm strapped to their wrists for most of their career and thought it the *norm,* it's even worse in the United Sates, where firearms are a way of life and readily available, this adds to the huge problem with returning veterans taking their own lives with a weapon, in 2012 6,500 former military personnel killed themselves, 177 serving soldiers also committed suicide, most of the 177 would have been by using their own issued weapon.

*****

Once I was released from custody, I began to live in my own world, I had lost another friend and Julie begged me to seek medical help, I wore combat gear and dog tags night and day, and began sleeping rough on the beach, digging myself in to the sand and pebbles, until the 'flu forced me back inside, I was losing my grip on reality.

I had also begun experiencing more and more 'flashbacks'. These had been around for a while, but were growing more frequent and intense the more stressed, depressed and sleep-deprived I became. Flashbacks very hard to explain to people who've never suffered from them. You're wide awake – mine almost always happened during the day – and your vision of the given incident is as clear and real as if you are really back there. At the same time, though, the rest of the world is there, too – it wasn't as though I was suddenly transported back to the Falklands. Part of my brain knew the flashback was in my imagination, but the rest of me couldn't help reacting as I would if it wasn't: my heartbeat would go mad, my adrenalin would surge and I'd either want to hide or fight or cry.

I had a variety but the most common was of an air attack. I would see – as clear as day, for a split second – a white Argentinean navy Sky Hawk streaking towards me. The cockpit area was like a huge pilot's helmet, with the pilot staring at me. He was bombing me and I was shooting at him and, to my ears, the air would be filled with the shriek of jet engines, close, low and at full power. Then it would be gone.

Dave to his credit took full responsibility for the incident with the gun and told the police it had nothing to do with me and he was sentenced to two years in prison, this added to my sense of guilt, that I should have done more to help him. I know he was a grown man, but I should have told him not to be so stupid, I had to bear some responsibility, as they say hindsight is a wonderful thing.

I didn't talk to Julie a lot – when I did, it was rambling or incoherent, talking about death and suicide, and the black hole of my future, our future. One minute I'd be shouting at her, the next I'd be curled up, crying, in a ball on the floor. She was tremendously strong, considering that she was pregnant with my unborn son.

I'M A SOLDIER

Julie arranged an appointment for me to see a counsellor in early 1994. At first, I refused to go – it was all bullshit, what did they know? So she gave me an ultimatum: if I didn't seek medical help, she would be forced to leave me.

At first, even the threat of Julie leaving didn't bother me, as the feelings of suicide had grown stronger. But some day's things didn't seem so bad and on one of those days I plucked up the courage to see a counsellor with Julie. It didn't work out brilliantly at first for lots of reasons, all of them to do with me. For a start, my depressed state had made me very selfish and I couldn't see the mental anguish my pregnant wife was enduring. And I couldn't talk about my problems, either. The counsellor, a lady called Kath Kelly, tried hard but I just clammed up.

I'm a soldier; I can sort this out myself, piece of piss. Next!

I listened while Julie told Kath about my mood swings and depression, about how I had stood on top of a bridge overlooking the sea, drunk and threatening to jump, about the hosepipe she had found in the boot of my car, the endless, horrible catalogue of violent and irrational behaviour that she had noticed, and put up with, in the seven years that she had known me.

Kath listened hard and focused straight away on the Falklands War, probing, asking questions, looking for clues, trying to elicit more information from me. It didn't make a lot of sense to me. The Falklands had ended a dozen years ago… what had that got to do with how I was now? She might as well have been talking to a boulder but she seemed to think she was getting somewhere. At the end of the session, she told me, 'I think we can help you, but I need you to see a psychiatrist to be sure. Since you're finding it difficult to talk about your experiences, I'd like you to go away and write down all your thoughts and feelings in a diary which we'll show to the psychiatrist.'

I took her advice and this book, ultimately, is the result.

I am extremely grateful to Kath for her understanding and compassion. When I read the insane rantings I committed to paper in those early days, it's as if another person wrote them, someone at least two rounds short of a full mag. In some ways, that is true.

Here are some of them.

(Some entries from my diary, 1994)

- Session with Counsellor this morning. She's asked me to write down my experiences for her, and she's sorting me out some proper, professional help.

- Dreamt I had a rat in my mouth last night. Disgusting.

- I had a night terror, in which I thought I saw a gremlin-type creature in the corner growling at me. I woke up terrified and covered in sweat and couldn't get back to sleep.

- Bad night terrors. A creature was after me. Got my rifle to kill it. It really scared Julie. I was running around the room screaming, lunging at things that weren't there. Julie made me go to the Doctor's and I'm taking tablets now. I hope they help but I don't know if it's worth living like this. I have to take one Seroxat table every day, and one Temazepam to help me sleep at night.

- Woke up in the middle of the night, as I do most nights. I say 'woke up' but the fact is I'm not really awake.

It's a weird state somewhere between being awake and asleep. The Temazepam aren't really helping all that much. I thought someone was stealing my watch. Then I thought I was having a heart attack, so I got up and started dialling 999, still in this half asleep state. Julie stopped me and calmed me down and persuaded me to get back to bed.

- I had an extremely bad night terror last night. I woke up and saw my arm severed on the bedside cabinet again.

- I'm starting to feel like my life is completely pointless. I'm just a burden and an embarrassment to everyone. I woke up during the night again and found I could not move. It was like I was paralysed. I had this sense of impending doom.

Despite me volunteering for the Northern Ireland tour, part of me is scared people think I'm just a coward. How can you be a soldier one second and the next a civilian and carry on as if nothing had happened.

Civvies ask you when you get home, 'Did you kill anyone?' What kind of a question is that? What answer do they want?

Mainly, I feel like a coward because I didn't fight hand-to-hand and I let those men die on the *Galahad*.

- Extremely bad night terror. I was having all the blood from my feet squeezed upwards towards my head. I was screaming like a banshee, convinced I was about to die when my head would explode. It took me about an hour for me to calm down. Thought my heart was going to stop – to me it was real.

At the moment I feel like I'm a worthless piece of rotting flesh. I am positive I would have been dead months ago if it was not for my wife. I take my anti-depressants and I am still depressed. I take my sleeping tablets so I can sleep and I don't frighten my wife half to death, but they don't always work. Why does she put up with me? I'm thirty-one but I feel more like ninety-one, and I've lost interest in everything. I can't even have a normal conversation any more. I really feel sorry for the soldiers who fought in World War One and had shell shock and were shot as cowards. Maybe some were cowards but many were not. I thought I was mentally very tough, a professional soldier. Was I wrong about myself all along?

- Another night terror. I was being held down by corpses, they pushed a grenade down my throat. I thought if I passed water it would pull the pin and detonate.

- Last night I had to get out of the house. I ended up sleeping on the beach in a trench. I felt almost like a corpse lying there. At about 02.30hrs I had a night terror. I felt like my tongue was being hacked out with bayonet. I stripped naked and ran into the sea, trying to drown myself in tide. It was too shallow so I went back to the trench and put my clothes back on.

- I think about the Falklands all the time now. Our boots were crap. They let water in and you could get trench foot. One soldier deliberately soaked his foot in water until it was so bad he had to be air lifted out of combat and his sock surgically removed. The Argies had better boots than ours, so when squaddies found a corpse they would take their boots off hoping they were the right size. Well, they didn't need them anymore. Some found boots with feet still in them and just squeezed the foot out and put it straight on. 9 Battery took photographs as they sat with their arms around corpses pretending to give them a cigarette. I didn't feel sorry for them at this time – that came much later, many years later. But some of the dead were children, sixteen year olds. Their bodies had limbs missing, whole heads missing, some still holding their rosary beads, with pictures of the Virgin Mary on their rifles. Their faces frozen in the horror of their own impending death. When I think of the smell of death I think of two smells. 1. The smell of rotting human flesh. 2. Opening the Rapier missile containers, smelling that sticky aroma. I can smell it now, kind of sweet.

- I don't know what to say. Another night terror. I woke and saw that all my internal organs had been torn out and put into a plastic bin liner.

I believe in the devil and evil. War is hell on earth, ongoing every day; even if you survive war the devil persecutes your mind for the rest of your life. But I'm very proud of what I did for my country.

I'm scared my son might be born dead. I fear I am teetering on the edge of insanity, if not already sliding down the hill. Why can't I take my own life? Because I am a coward. I have been sleeping outdoors a lot lately. I made a hide – it's funny how you somehow feel safer in the earth.

Things got no better after my son Aiden was born in the summer.

- I was sitting in a chair holding the baby when I suddenly started to get hot flushes and a pain in my chest. I got myself down to the doctors and they examined me and said it was just a panic attack brought on by this whole thing. I thought I was having a heart attack, but it wasn't that serious.

I feel very depressed and suicidal. I fantasise about walking into a crowded pub and putting a gun into my mouth and blowing my head off, or walk down Dalton Road on a busy shopping day, pouring a jerry can of petrol over myself and striking a match, so that I die like those Welsh Guardsmen I was supposed to be protecting. But then that's not fair on the innocent people. Why give them nightmares like mine? I am just one pathetic individual, why can't someone take me out at dawn and put this excuse for a human to death? I really embarrassed myself a couple of years ago. I went for a drink with a friend and his girlfriend. We were OK till we went into a night-club. The place was heaving, I felt closed in and paranoid. I remember thinking if a bomb goes off now, we're all dog meat. The strobe lights started flashing, it reminded me of incoming tracer rounds. I dropped my pint and just ran for the door. I was panic-stricken. If anyone had tried to stop me I would have torn their throats out to breathe fresh air. I wanted to be alone on top of a mountain.

- The depression is so bad it has taken on a physical presence like a nagging pain in my stomach.

If you were raped, I doubt you would want to watch videos about it, yet I watch war films and violent films all the time. I was told to write so I'm writing; I hope some good will come of it. I think I'll take my happy pill and vegetate now.

Thought about the *Sir Galahad* again. I imagined a burnt, limbless soldier saying 'Why didn't you fire? Why did you let my friends die?'

- I think about Northern Ireland a lot. The savagery in Northern Ireland knows no bounds but gets little publicity as the government likes to keep the lid on things. One glimpse by the media was the two soldiers driving the unmarked Q car who were murdered at the funeral. They took a wrong turn and were blocked in by a mob, beaten and finally executed by IRA murderers. The corpses lay strewn in the street, stripped naked like unwanted litter. A priest went to the scene to pray over the bodies, a man of God, not afraid or intimidated by the men of violence.

- I am totally irrelevant, better forgotten. My mind feels like a spinning wheel going out of control.

As I read it back to myself, I noticed a lot of my nightmares revolved around the *Sir Galahad*; there weren't many days, if any, that I didn't think about it. Maybe there was something in what Kath had said?

By night, the terrors continued, and by day my mind was full of thoughts of suicide and death. The depression developed to the point where I had a permanent headache and constant diarrhoea. I'd also become paranoid – every time I went out in my car, I would check underneath first for explosive devices, I checked all the post carefully before openings it, I was sure our telephone was bugged.

Unsurprisingly, my relationship with Julie – who had shown the patience of a saint – was falling apart.

I would go out drinking to get obliterated, a danger to others in that state as much as to myself. I half-wanted someone to start on me so that I could do them some serious damage, but people tended to give me a wide berth.

In some ways, I wished I'd lost a limb, a badge of suffering that people could see: no-one could see the damage inside my head. I remember thinking; *I should be preserved as some sort of exhibit so people can understand what war does to your mind.* The irony was that I had no regrets at all about having gone to the Falklands, or about joining the Army. I'd have been happy for Aiden to follow in my footsteps. I just regretted the things that had happened out there.

My first appointment with the psychiatrist, Dr Anthony Page, came around eventually. I wasn't looking forward to it: I didn't like talking about the state I was in, but Kath had obviously briefed him about me; he held out his hand for the blue journal I'd been keeping and there was a long and uncomfortable silence as he read every word, letting it all sink in.

After he'd finished, he closed the book with a thoughtful nod and handed it back to me. Then he began to ask me a series of questions.

Did I feel suicidal?

How long had this all been going on?

What form did my nightmares take?

Was I sleeping properly?

Did I think about the Falklands a lot?

He was calm and thoughtful, carefully writing down my answers as I spoke.

After 20 minutes or so, he sat back and clasped his fingers together.

'I'm confident you are suffering from Post-Traumatic Stress Disorder,' he said. He went on to explain that this was a condition discovered in 1980 in the USA during a study on Vietnam veterans which had examined the high levels of psychiatric problems and mental illness many of them had experienced after that war. Some excellent treatments had been developed which meant that it was possible for it to be cured completely, or certainly reduced in intensity.

This was amazing news: Dr Page knew what my problems were, and he knew how to cure them. I felt a weight lift off me.

He told me I would be working with a community psychiatric nurse called Frank Quegan, who had a particular interest in PTSD. Then he gave me another appointment to see him, we shook hands and I left.

As I was considered to be at high risk of suicide, I continued seeing Kath until my treatment with Frank started. Among the medication I was prescribed was another antidepressant drug called clomipramine. I'd gone from being someone who rarely too so much as an aspirin to a walking medicine cabinet.

The clomapramine was designed to help me sleep, and it did reduce the night terrors but the side effects were awful; I felt sick constantly, and completely knackered. I slept for most of the time and when I was awake I was like a zombie. I became even more withdrawn, retreating into my shell for hours on end, not speaking or interacting with anyone. Keeping my eyes open and focused was a chore. One day, I drove my car into a fence by accident, and it says a lot that no-one was at all surprised. I didn't have the energy to smash the house up or become aggressive towards Julie, but her quality of life was nil, as was mine.

I suppose it was fitting that the day I had to start my treatment with Frank I'd been sleeping on the beach. I was dressed normally – by my eccentric standards: month-old combats covered in mud and fragments of shale. It was only when I made my way back home in the morning, looking like Rambo's wild-eyed, feral cousin, that Julie reminded me I had an appointment. I didn't have time to change or even wash, and I think Frank was mildly concerned that I might have an AK47 stuck under my camouflage jacket. I was actually as surprised at his appearance: he was a young man in his late twenties, with shoulder-length, curly hair, a complete contrast to Dr Page.

I had expected him to focus on the war straight away, but he never mentioned it. First, he had me fill out a Beck's Depression Inventory, a questionnaire developed by a US psychiatrist to assess your mental state. I scored 49 out of 63, which indicated severe depression.

Next, he asked me to make a verbal contract with him that I would not harm myself.

For the next eight months, I worked with Frank on my problems. I attended anger management courses, and my depression decreased until I got it down to 7/63 on the Beck's scale – a huge improvement, and one which put me in line with most of the population.

Most startling of all, Frank cured my flashbacks, using a method developed in Israel to help soldiers suffering from mental problems related to combat stress. When he outlined it to me I was sceptical to say the least. It seemed too simple. He wanted me to imagine the flashback in my mind and then to think of a positive statement. For instance, I would think of fighter-bomber jets flying overhead and say, *'I am proud to have done my duty.'* Meanwhile, Frank would move his finger slowly, from left to right, with my eyes following it as I repeated my statement.

To my amazement, it only took about half a dozen of these exercises to stop the flashbacks. I've not had one since. Even Frank admitted he didn't know how exactly how it worked, but who cares? It works.

It's extremely important to build up a relationship with someone like Frank and I believe I did that. It seemed to me that he was putting so much effort into my problems that I had to give him something back in return. So in the early days, when he asked me how I was doing, I'd say I was OK, when really – though I was improving – I was still in a dreadful state.

Luckily, Julie would tell him the truth, forcing me to be honest, and we made progress.

Unfortunately, the night terrors continued, as they do to this day, but I went from a man who slept on the beach, thought constantly of suicide and wouldn't admit his problems to anyone other than his wife to someone who – eventually – felt able to tell the world.

During one of our sessions, Frank gave me the address of an ex-services charity which had homes around the country to help former soldiers and others with their problems. I talked it through with Julie and she decided to give them a call; they ended up sending a Flight Lieutenant down to assess me. He suggested I spend some time at a residential place in Scotland – he sold it to me by making it sound like Butlins for ex-squaddies. I'd be there for a fortnight, with the chance of a return visit later. I was a little apprehensive – I still found it hard discussing my situation with people I didn't know – but at least there would be other ex-squaddies there, guys like me to whom I could relate. I could see that chatting to men who were going through the same things could be a great benefit.

The only problem was the funding. I had no war pension and no job, so I had to apply to the Social Services for the money. The social services sent a lady round to assess me and after a couple of hours of the Spanish Inquisition she closed her folder and said I had no chance. She was right. I got a letter a week or so later saying that Cumbria Social Services had overspent their budget for the year. This was a massive blow: having got over the mental hurdle of agreeing to go to north in the first place, I'd started looking forward to it, hoping it might be good for me. I was angry and down about it, and it reminded of Rudyard Kipling's famous lines:

For it's Tommy this, an' Tommy that, an' "Chuck him out, the brute!"

But it's "Saviour of 'is country," when the guns begin to shoot;

An' it's Tommy this, an' Tommy that, an' anything you please;

But Tommy ain't a bloomin' fool - you bet that Tommy sees!

As it turned out, my war pension wasn't far off, so that funded the trip instead. Sadly, it turned out to be a waste of money.

I could have had a rail warrant to get up there but Scouse volunteered to take me in his car. That was good of him; I didn't really want to go alone. I wish I'd never accepted his offer. After about a three hour drive, we eventually reached the place. We drove down a long dark driveway and Scouse started to smirk. Out of the mist appeared an old building, like something out of *Psycho*.

'What the hell is this?' I said, as Scouse's smirk broke into a sick giggle. In about five seconds flat, he'd stopped the car, jumped out, got my bag out of the boot, told me to give him a bell if I needed anything and disappeared in a cloud of gravel and exhaust fumes. The bastard, I'd have done the same thing. I picked up my Army holdall and decided to see if Lurch was in. As I neared the large wooden doors I peered through the windows and could see a semi-circle of high-backed geriatric chairs: it reminded me of the home that my mother had recently moved to. This was a mistake, and it wasn't as if I could just hop on a bus. I was hundreds of miles away from Julie and the baby.

I was met by the matron, who looked surprised I could still walk without the aid of a zimmer frame. She took my medication from me and told me the meal times.

'So you have Post Traumatic Stress Disorder?' she said, looking a bit mystified. That wasn't a great start.

It got worse when she showed me to my room; I was sharing with another bloke, which was bad news given my night terrors.

I went downstairs for a brew and to see who else was there. It turned out I was just about the only Englishman in the place, which probably explained why the rest of the residents, most of them older than me and Scots or northern Irish, tended to look at me like I had two heads. One of the care attendants pointed me in the direction of a lad who was around my age. He turned out to be another Falklands veteran, an ex-Scots Guard who knew Wilbour. Small world. He was another PTSD sufferer: he told me how his marriage had collapsed and he was living on his own, and generally looked about as low and depressed as I felt. The whole thing was a waste of time, he said: he'd been there a couple of days and was going home at the weekend, a week early. I watched *Wheel Of Fortune* in a TV room, had another brew, a bath and hit the sack.

I said goodnight to my roommate – a softly-spoken ex-RAF chap from Northern Ireland – and got my head down. I woke with a start at around 2am and, for once, it wasn't down to a nightmare. The place was suddenly alive with the sound of loud, drunken voices, crashing and banging around and then a stereo going on at full volume. I buried my head in my pillow, but the guys outside started banging on our door, then opening it, shouting and then slamming it again.

Complaining to them was out of the question – there were half a dozen of them, they were smashed and wouldn't have taken kindly to it. I tried to ignore them, and eventually they drifted away, after throwing up, loudly and repeatedly, in the toilet next to my room.

Some treatment for PTSD this was. I lay awake all night, angry and depressed and resolved to leave as soon as possible. Julie arranged for a lift so after a bowl of porridge I walked down the lane to the river at the bottom and took in the fresh air. The countryside was beautiful, but I live near beautiful countryside in the Lake District and this place was making me more stressed and paranoid than I'd been before.

I escaped around lunchtime, when a mate of mine drove all the way from Barrow to get me. Later, I wrote to the charity explaining why I'd left. They wrote back, expressing their regret and offering me a further two weeks there, which suggested they had somewhat missed the point. I'm sure it worked for others, but it was only going to make me worse.

THE COURT CASE

Sadly, although I was getting a lot closer to normality than I'd been in my darkest days, my marriage was at an end. Julie left me, and I can't really blame her. I'd put her through the mill over the last decade or so.

The stress of the break-up and the subsequent divorce didn't help my mental state, but with help from Dr Page and Frank Quegan I just about held it together.

In 1998 I started going out with a local girl called Rebecca and after a couple of years we were married. It wasn't long before Bex became pregnant with our daughter Annabelle. Happy days, at the time, she is fourteen years old now and I see her regularly.

My night terrors were still coming, though they were less frequent and frightening as the years wore on, and I knew I would never escape them.

I was still haunted by memories of the *Sir Galahad*, but had gradually come round to the idea that it wasn't my entire fault; the equipment had malfunctioned, and the Guards shouldn't even have been aboard the ship when the attack happened anyway. Others could share at least some of the blame.

But I had no realistic hope of finding work. I wasn't even 40, but I was washed up and finished. It was a depressing thought.

Then one day I got chatting to another ex-soldier who had also been diagnosed with PTSD; he told me that a class action was being developed in order that victims could sue the Ministry of Defence for damages. The basis of the action was that the MoD had known all along that soldiers were likely to suffer psychological injury from the conflict, that they'd known how to help them with this and that they had failed to do so.

I didn't know what a class action was – it turned out to be a group of people all suing together to avoid the cost and repetition of hundreds of individual cases – but I was very interested: not so much by the idea of financial compensation, though obviously that would have been handy, but mainly because I wanted someone, somewhere, to recognise what had happened to me and others like me.

I decided to seek legal advice, and, after bouncing around a number of different solicitors, I found myself represented by the firm taking the lead in the PTSD case, Manchester-based Linder Myers.

I underwent what felt like dozens of interviews and evaluations, including a very thorough psychiatric investigation carried out by Dr Jonathan Bisson, an expert in PTSD, a leading lecturer in psychiatry and a former Army psychiatrist. I remember him telling me that I had had a window of opportunity for treatment of my PTSD after the Falklands War; if you catch it early enough, it can be dealt with to the point where it can often be cured. Unfortunately, due to the long period that had elapsed between the end of the war and my eventual diagnosis, that window of opportunity was now closed. 'I'm afraid you will have varying degrees of PTSD for the rest of your life,' he said. Not great news, but it was good that he at least recognised my problem. Before the Falklands, I'd been fine; the condition had developed 'as a direct result' said his report.

Another psychiatric evaluation was done in Manchester by an American Professor, Charles Figley. I had confidence that Charles really understood PTSD and combat stress generally because, uniquely for an expert in this field, as far as I know, his experience was not limited to what you could read in textbooks. He had spent four years in the United States Marine Corps between 1963 and 1967, and among that period was a whole year spent fighting in Vietnam. He put me at my ease immediately and we spent several hours together which ended when he shared some relaxation techniques which did help to calm me down. He, too, said categorically that my problems were 'combat-related.'

I had another psychiatric evaluation carried out in Edinburgh and that, again, confirmed the same thing – I had a bad case of PTSD brought on by the events I'd witnessed in the Falklands.

Not surprisingly, this was disputed by the Government. I had a further evaluation, carried out in Liverpool for the MoD by a Dr Steven O'Brien. He argued that I didn't have PTSD after all. The jist of his argument centred on the ad that I had posted in *Soldier Of Fortune* magazine advertising my services as a mercenary, and the fact that I had later re-enlisted in the Army and then volunteered for service in Northern Ireland. This showed I didn't avoid stressful situations and danger, he said; in fact,

I actually sought them out. This meant, he felt, that the PTSD diagnosis was incorrect.

This ignored the fact that many other sufferers had done exactly that kind of thing – and also that I wasn't aware, at the time that I re-enlisted, of exactly what my problem was.

Linder Myers also took witness statements from people who could confirm the changes in me after the Falklands. From the Army side, they interviewed Edward 'Scouse' Denmark, Bob Pearson and three other lads who had all served with me down there.

My dad and even one of our neighbours back home also gave statements. I was and still am very grateful for the support of all of these people. Their statements make sober reading for me.

Scouse said I was 'like a zombie, numb and withdrawn' when he saw me in Stanley after the ceasefire; he told how he'd pulled me back from the railings on the ship on the way home and how I'd been crying uncontrollably about the two Argentinean pilots I felt sure I had killed.

He went into detail about rooming with me for two years during my second spell in the Army, saying he had heard second-hand tales of my night terrors after the end of the war but that during the years we shared a room, he'd seen them for himself: 'I experienced at first hand, on the majority of nights, occasions when he would often wake up screaming and retching as though he was choking on an object. He would also sit up whilst still asleep and say there was someone in the room. He would often imagine there was an Indian warrior or Roman soldier.'

He went on: 'Before going to the Falklands, Tony was regarded as being a popular, easy going and enthusiastic member of our unit. He had a reputation of being a very good Rapier missile operator. He was also very conscientious about his dress and he had a high level of fitness. After returning (we) were well aware of his unstable nature. Within the Regiment there is a hierarchy based on the toughest men. Because of Tony's violent reputation, even these men tended to steer clear of him. Tony had become noticeably more violent and destructive (and) was generally regarded as being a 'lunatic' by the other lads.'

It wasn't a flattering read, but it did at least paint a picture of the changes in me since the Falklands.

Bob – the sergeant in charge of 32 Alpha – described me as 'a very keen and professional young soldier' who might have been promoted if I'd stayed in the Army. He said I'd become 'much quieter and withdrawn' after the *Sir Galahad* sinking.

Pete Ball, our unit's medic, said that despite all of this, and despite the fact that I was physically assessed after the conflict ended, 'no time was given to (my) psychological and emotional state of mind'.

Even if it had been, however, and PTSD had been diagnosed, he said it would have made no difference. 'Had I reported this to his superior officers, none of them would have cared. Our superiors classed people reporting psychological problems as 'working their ticket' and putting their symptoms on.'

He talked about noticing the change in me after I re-enlisted. 'I had less contact with Anthony because I had moved further up the ranks. (But) he was different compared to the Anthony I had known before the

Falklands. He had no sparkle in his mannerisms. He appeared to be distant and withdrawn a lot of the time.

'I believe Anthony would have had the potential to go high up in the Army had he not been affected by his experiences in the Falklands. He was a good soldier before the Falklands.'

My dad's statement, confirmed by a neighbour, went into some detail about my violent outbursts at home. 'Prior to joining the Army, there was nothing aggressive or abnormal about him. On his return from the Falklands War, he had undergone a total character change. From being a normal, happy-go-lucky lad, he had turned into a drunken, loud-mouthed, violent thug who on a number of occasions smashed up my home and threatened his family and friends. Whilst on leave he took to sleeping in a trench in the garden in his uniform and on occasions chased people in the street.

'In my opinion, the person who went to the Falklands and the person who returned are two different people. I feel I lost my boy in the war, only he didn't die. I fear it is only a matter of time before he takes his own life and finally gets some peace.'

My second wife, Rebecca, also gave a statement in which she confirmed my regular night terrors and panic attacks.

With all of that behind me, and despite the report by the MoD's Dr O'Brien, I felt reasonably confident that we had a chance of winning: no-one could realistically claim I was making up my symptoms, they clearly only started after the Falklands and – far from the Army doing anything to help – the prevailing attitude was, at best, to ignore mental health issues.

With time on my hands as we waited for the case to come to court, I started looking deeper into PTSD.

What is it? It's a psychiatric disorder that can occur when you experience life-threatening events. Military combat – such as that I saw in the Falklands – is only one form of this. PTSD can be triggered by going through natural disasters, or getting caught up in terrorist incidents or serious accidents. A woman might suffer it following a violent assault, like a rape. A fire fighter might suffer it after finding a small child dead in a house fire.

In the military context, it has certainly been around as long as warfare, and there are discussions of similar conditions in ancient literature. The beginning of the modern understanding of PTSD dates from the time of the American Civil War. Men suffering emotional problems after that extremely vicious conflict were said to have 'soldier's heart' or 'Da Costa's Syndrome'. In the First World War, it was called 'shell shock'. By the time the Second World War came around, it was more often called 'combat fatigue'.

The proper research and documentation of PTSD began in earnest after the Vietnam War and it has subsequently been observed in all veteran populations which have been studied, including those of World War II, the Korean conflict, the two Gulf Wars, the Falklands, Northern Ireland Afghanistan and in United Nations peacekeeping forces deployed to war zones around the world.

What are the symptoms? Well, lots of them were familiar to me. If you have PTSD, you will often relive the 'trigger' experiences through nightmares and flashbacks. You can have difficulty sleeping, you might feel detached from everyday life and you can also suffer physical symptoms: headaches, stomach complaints, problems with your immune system, dizziness, chest and general pain are common. It is often accompanied by depression, memory loss, drink or drug abuse, an inability to hold down jobs and the collapse of marriages, family life and other relationships.

How do you cure PTSD? The good news about the disorder is that it can be treated – if you catch it early enough. It varies from case to case, but it has been known for a long time that a mixture of medication and therapy, applied as soon as possible after the traumatic events, have positive outcomes. Clearly, the Army couldn't haul me off the battlefield for a nice psychiatric chat followed by a handful of anti-depressants within an hour of the *Sir Galahad* tragedy. For starters, they had lads with arms and legs missing who needed dealing with first. But they could have had me seen to after the cessation of hostilities – after all, the MoD had sent a team of Royal Navy psychiatrists down to the Falklands with the task force. It was years later before I got any help and I never got any from the Army.

Does every combat veteran suffer from PTSD? Thankfully, no, though that creates difficulties for those who do. In 1988, a major US study revealed that 30% of veterans experienced the disorder at some point since returning from Vietnam. While that is a very large number, it still means 70% did not. This means the sceptics – and there are many, in and out of uniform – have the ammunition to help them to deny it's a real problem.

The Government, for instance, was fighting the court case, and it was obvious why. If they admitted that PTSD existed – or, more importantly – that they could and should have done something about it in my case and in hundreds of others, this would throw the doors open to compensation claims from all suffering veterans from that period and any conflict since the Falklands (the period during which it was reasonable to expect the government to act to help soldiers). Potentially, the bill would run into hundreds of millions of pounds.

It wasn't just those with a vested interest who had their doubts: others just can't understand how anyone could suffer from PTSD. After all, their granddad was in World War Two… he fought the Germans for five years and he's alright, isn't he? If I had a pound for every time I've heard this argument, I'd be a rich man, and my response is always the same. Firstly, how do you know your granddad is alright? It's hardly news that the stiff upper lip mentality prevalent in those of earlier generations means many keep their emotions firmly in check. Secondly, maybe your granddad is one of the lucky majority. As I say, not every combat soldier will end up suffering from PTSD; in fact, most don't. Many of the lads who fought in the Falklands saw and did far worse things than me and came away mentally unscathed. Why is that? I wish I knew, but no-one does, not even the experts.

I can understand why it's a controversial area for so many people. After all, you can see the damage to a soldier who has stood on a land mine, or been badly burned; you can't see inside a man's head and see what has gone wrong in there. Naturally enough, some people think it's faked, or exaggerated, or imagined.

Some people were particularly annoyed by the fact that PTSD-suffering veterans were trying to claim financial compensation. If I had another pound for every time I've heard, *'Well, no-one forced you to join the Army... it goes with the territory,'* I wouldn't just be rich,

I'd be writing this somewhere warm, sunny and tropical, rather than rainy old Cumbria.

I was always struck by the unfairness of this.

You don't hear people complaining when the fire-fighter is compensated for the horror of finding the child's body, or the policeman for seeing someone commit suicide. Why is it different for soldiers? It's right to say that no-one forced me to join the Army. I joined because I'd always wanted to be a soldier, and I'd join again if I had my time again. I accept, also, that all soldiers know that they may be going to war – more so now than in my day – and that that 'goes with the territory'. However, PTSD doesn't have to be a part of that. As I've said, it's not incurable, as long as you take it seriously and treat it early.

We were to be represented in the High Court by Stephen Irwin QC. Three months before the case went to court, I got to meet Irwin in person because mine had been identified as a 'lead case' in the action. It had now been joined by hundreds of other ex-servicemen – among them, ironically, were 40 or so of the lads who'd been aboard the *Sir Galahad*. I was asked to attend a meeting with the QC and other members of his team. It turned out to be a rather dispiriting waste of time, and one that completely wrecked my confidence in our case. I was ushered in to a meeting room, where Irwin sat at a table, flicking through my files, his reading glasses balanced on the end of his nose. He did not acknowledge me, and I waited for what seemed like hours as he and his colleagues grunted and sighed and ploughed through their reams of paperwork. After a while, he looked up and asked me asked if I had anything to say.

'Yes,' I said. 'If we lose the case, are you going to appeal? Maybe take the case to the European Court of Human Rights?'

He cleared his throat. 'If we lose then I'm afraid that's it,' he said. 'I certainly will not making an appeal. It will be over.'

This and – rightly or wrongly – his general demeanour did not fill me with any enthusiasm; from that day on, I had a gut feeling we would lose.

In the end, it took seven years for the case to come to court, with the big day rolling around on March 4, 2002. It was scheduled to last eight months, which gives you some idea of why lawyers tend to live in nice, big houses, though it didn't take anywhere near as long as that. I was looking forward to my big day, to the chance to tell my story and fight my corner but, in the end, I was never even called to give evidence. They seem to have been worried that it may have been too traumatic for some veterans to give evidence. I can accept that – everyone is different – but I didn't feel that way. As it was, my evidence was rubbished in a rebuttal statement for the MoD by Colonel Graham Smith – my old friend GBH, the former Major who had been our Battery commander during the Falklands. He described my statement as being, variously, inaccurate, exaggerated and 'disingenuous'. I had to look the last one up – my dictionary defines it as 'Not straightforward or candid; insincere or calculating.' In layman's terms, a lying bastard. I didn't have the opportunity to defend myself against that, sadly; I'd have liked to because it was very unfair.

As the case dragged on, all I could do was ring Linder Myers each week to find out how things were progressing. The people on the other end never sounded all that optimistic, not that they could really tell me anything. The thrust of it always seemed to be that there were problems with 'generic issues' in our case. That meant nothing to me but I crossed my fingers and waited by the phone.

We had got a boost the week before the trial started, when it was announced that the former director General of the Army Medical Service was to give evidence against the Ministry of Defence on our behalf.

The BBC reported this dramatic twist as follows:

Major General Robin Short, who planned Britain's medical deployment in the Gulf War, is to be a witness in a case against the MoD next week.

The 1,900 claimants are making a joint action which will be dealt with in one generic court case.

There are many who have been left severely mentally disabled by their experiences.

They claim the MoD failed to treat them properly for PTSD, a disorder which is common in situations of war and conflict.

Maj Gen Short told BBC Radio 4's Today programme that soldiers should have had better support from their former employer.

'When one looks on an individual case basis there is no doubt there are many who have been left severely

mentally disabled by their experiences and by the way they were treated thereafter,' he told the programme.

'I have no doubt that more could have been done. And secondly there is no doubt in my mind that more should be and needs to be done even now.

'We should have been able to not accept that this was normal, we should have looked at it then and thought what should we be doing to identify what can we do to help these people.'

Maj Gen Short said he was aware of the repercussions of such a senior officer giving evidence against the MoD, but he said he had tried to raise the matter when he was in service and 'received no support'.

He added that he believed people currently serving in Afghanistan were being similarly affected.

The men bringing the action against the MoD at the High Court served in Northern Ireland, Bosnia, the Falklands and the Gulf.

Solicitor Mark McGhee, of Linder Myers which is representing the veterans, said PTSD 'destroys lives'.

'The servicemen feel the MoD didn't do enough to educate them or to treat them when they'd developed PTSD

and as a result their health deteriorated and they don't have much of a life,' he said.

The MoD said that while it could not comment on the court case, it recognised that some members of the armed forces did suffer stress after traumatic experiences.

A spokesman added that the department had a 'duty' to ensure that they received 'proper treatment and if they did not, they 'may be entitled to compensation'.

I don't know about you, but to me that sounded like a nail in the Government's coffin.

Sadly, my optimism was short-lived.

On May 21, Mr Justice Owen ruled in favour of the MoD. In his judgement, he said: 'It has long been recognised that combat may result in psychiatric as well as physical casualties. The infliction of shock and extreme stress on an enemy has been a military objective throughout history. War and warlike operations inevitably take their toll, both physical and psychological.'

That didn't mean, apparently, that those in charge needed to give much of a toss about the people at the sharp end.

Linder Myers issued a statement afterwards.

The Claimants volunteered for a life that they knew might mean combat and conflict, and exposure to the shocking events of war. They willingly accepted the risks of their service; but they relied on the MoD to care for them properly. As the MoD themselves put it in their Claims Annual Report 2001/2: "...this litigation is not about the validity of PTSD as a psychiatric disorder, nor is it about soldiers unjustifiably suing for being exposed to traumatic incidents while serving in HM Forces. The Claimants' case is that PTSD is detectable and preventable, and that proper systems would or should have achieved these objectives in the vast majority of cases."

The Court in this judgment accepts the reality and severity of the psychological injuries of war. But the result of the trial means that only a fraction of the soldiers, sailors and airmen we represent will be able to recover compensation. Many will not, because the Court found that the MoD can take the benefit of a statutory immunity which applied up to 1987. Others cannot recover because of a further historical immunity, which the judge has found still applies, for things done well away from any live military action. While the judge found there was effective treatment available during almost all of the period covered by this litigation, he did not find that the MoD had a duty to identify sufferers, so as to be able to treat them.

We are very disappointed by these findings. The clear implication is that the onus was on the individual to make known their own suffering, even where they were untrained and ignorant of the nature and cause of their problems.

We are also dismayed by the findings as to what the MoD actually knew – and what they should have known – about the long-term psychological consequences of war, which often do not surface until long after the shooting has stopped. These consequences include Post Traumatic Stress Disorder, depression and anxiety, often accompanied by alcohol abuse, unemployment, family break-up, offending, homelessness and even suicide.

We believe that much of the evidence in the case, and in the documents we analysed, show that long term consequences have been known about for many years. We believe it was also shown that the state of British military psychiatry was woeful during the 1970s and unsatisfactory in the 1980s and 1990s. That has been reflected in the judgment only on some specific points, where the judge has found the MoD were in breach of their duty of care to the men. Those points are important, but not nearly wide enough.

The judge conducted this trial in an extremely courteous way. In particular, he showed great kindness to many distressed witnesses who still suffer in their minds from the effects of war or terrorist action. We are grateful to him for that. But we cannot accept that some of his most important findings as to what the military should have known and should have done are correct. Taken together, we believe these findings have the effect of relieving the military of responsibilities it is their duty to bear. We are therefore considering an appeal.

This case was always about much more than simply compensation for affected individuals. From the outset, it was the Claimants' intention to bring the mental scars of war into the open and onto the public agenda. They wanted to try and ensure that future generations of service personnel will not have these problems ignored or side-lined, as in the past. Here we believe the case has succeeded and will succeed in focussing attention on this suffering, as never before.

British forces are severely overstretched and under-resourced. Within the past two years alone, they have been deployed abroad in substantial campaigns in Afghanistan and Iraq. Some of the servicemen and women involved will have returned with psychological injuries, which may not surface for some time – quite often for years. The public must realise this is not a fanciful notion but reality. On the MoD's own figures, and depending on the nature of the campaign, between 5 and 40% of all casualties are psychiatric casualties. It is imperative that the military establishment and the government take this problem seriously now, and look out for these victims who have served their country and suffered for it. In the light of the judgment, they have a clear obligation to treat them and support them adequately, whether or not they remain in the forces. We do not want to be in court in another ten years, making the same arguments for another generation, as we have made for those who fought and suffered in the Falklands, Northern Ireland, the First Gulf War and Bosnia.

I think that sums it up very well; it was never, for me, really about money. I wanted someone to put their hands up and say, *Sorry, we could have done more.*

As much as anything, we all wanted to raise the profile of PTSD and put the military in a position where they had to do something to protect other servicemen and women in the future going through what we'd experienced.

It was a blow, the collapse of the court case. Scouse and I handed our campaign medals back into 10 Downing Street in protest and resigned ourselves to the fact that we were going no further. But I feel we did at least get PTSD into the public eye.

REQUIEM FOR A SOLDIER

In 2007 I had the chance for an emotional return to the Falkland Islands for the 25th Anniversary Pilgrimage, speaking to veterans that had gone back since the War they all said it was a positive thing and helped them put some of their ghosts to rest, especially those that were suffering from mental health issues, but I was unsure myself and slightly apprehensive, but I put my name down with SAMA 82, along with another veteran from my Regiment and waited to see if we were both successful as I had already decided I would only go if Edward (Scouse Denmark) was coming with me.

Looking at it from a therapeutic point of view, I took the view that it may be worth the long journey down south and like the rest of the lads waited to see if our names had been pulled from the hat, plus going back with a close friend and fellow soldier from my Regiment also made it an easier decision.

Right from the offset things became complicated and controversial, when were told by the Pilgrimage organisers that nobody was guaranteed a seat on the plane, myself and Edward looked into other options of making our own way down to the Falklands, so I decided to make a phone call to RAF Brize Norton and inquire about the cost to pay for a flight myself with the RAF on one of their flights that are usually half empty.

I was pleasantly shocked and stunned when I was told by a female operator that it would cost me £45,obviously assumed she was mistaken asked several times and she told confirmed the price was correct and gave me a telephone number to book the flight. Gobsmacked I immediately rang Edward, we were both overjoyed at the news and Edward rang up to book our flight. Like the old saying goes, if something seems too good to be true it usually is and Eddy rang me back to tell me that he rang the number and was told the cost would be £1,400 each.

We were both back to square one, I was very sad, but when Edward told me that if were civil servants we could still go for £45, I became angry, a civil servant who works in a tax office for arguments sake who has no connection to the military can if they want fly back to the Falklands for £45. Myself and Edward and any other Falkland's veterans would have to stump up £1,400, which just can't be right by anyone's standards surely? I immediately contacted the then Veterans minister The Right Honourable Derek Twigg at the MOD and my local MP, The Right Honourable John Hutton. Derek Twigg would also be making the trip for the Pilgrimage on a different flight.

After I had posted this information on my Blog, I received a very angry shouty phone call from one of the Pilgrimage organisers who was not very happy and told me I was 'Out of order', I agreed something was very out of order and it was not me and told him in an equally angry colourful exchange, the time for being screamed at by Sergeant Majors was long gone.

After I slammed the phone down it seemed obvious to me that my chances of going back to the Falklands with SAMA (82) were dead in the water. As I'm typing this in 2016, in an article in the Times newspaper by Catherin Philip June 18th the headline reads, *Widows pay £2,200 to visit Falkland's war graves.* Things don't seem to have got any better with the passing of time.

You can imagine my utter surprise and astonishment when both of our names were eventually chosen for a seat and Edward drove us both to London and the aptly named *Union Jack Club*, an Armed Forces club/hotel in central London for members and veterans of the British Armed Services.

Going through the main doors with my bags I felt like I was back in the army, as we had to confirm who we were the usual name, rank, number, Regiment routine, I was just waiting for someone to give me a sweeping brush. The atmosphere was jovial and pleasant, lots of laughter and back slapping as comrades who had not seen each other for twenty five years shared memories good and bad and funny, the larger groups of Scots Guards and Para's and Royal Marines were getting stuck into the bar as per normal.

Finding my room I dropped my bags, had a wash in the shared Victorian bathrooms, located in the corridor, which were reminiscent of a military by gone era and went back down to the bar area and had a couple a beers and a chat with some of the lads from my Regiment that were also going back, they seemed very excited and were telling me which Falkland Island families they were staying with.

I had decided that I did not want to stay with a family, due to my PTSD and nightmares and felt more comfortable staying in a porta cabin at an army camp. Edward also agreed, this was no reflection on the generosity of the Islanders and was a decision based purely on my night-time outbursts of screaming and shouting in my sleep, which I particularly did not want the young children of these families to witness.

Edward left the bar first after about an hour and I soon followed him after a couple of beers and a glimpse of Margaret Thatcher who was enveloped in a scrum of handshaker's and had another terrible night's sleep, part of me wanted the organisers to say there had been a mistake and then I could feign annoyance and go home to my partner Linda who I had never been apart from since we met, but I tossed and turned sweating and shouting , realizing I had now committed and I didn't want to let Edward down, thinking like a serving soldier again. I felt like I had no choice and I had to go, like it or not, it was like doing another army course that I had to pass, and to pass this one I had to get on those buses tomorrow, like the buses that took us to War in 1982 and return to somewhere that had a detrimental effect and consumed my life negatively for the last twenty five years. You have had your orders now McNally I thought to myself, *so man up and get on with it.*

Bright and early next morning we were off, it took a couple of hours to take us down the motorway to Gatwick airport, the coaches buzzed with exuberant chatter and laughter until some drifted off, to sleep off last night's alcohol, I had done many trips like this on buses full of soldiers, not quite as old in years as this bunch and usually wearing my uniform on occasion carrying a rifle, the nearest I could compare it to was when we went skiing in Germany on Exercise *Snow queen.* Another big difference this time we would be flying with a civilian airline *Monarch* and not the usual RAF VC10, plus this was a very mixed group of ex-servicemen from all of the branch's, that shared a common bond, we had all been part of the liberation of the Falklands Islands and were holders of the South Atlantic Medal (with rosette).

Compared to the arduous stomach churning eight weeks at sea it took us to get there in 1982, the almost twenty hours with a stop off in Brazil, was luxury, the aircraft had the feel of a holiday flight at times and we remembered all the good experiences we had together and I started to relax into the whole Pilgrimage idea, that was until we were only around four hours from our destination when we were suddenly confronted by a lady holding a photograph album, it was full of photographs of her young son, tears were streaming down her face as she shows us the pictures, she had them right from when he was a baby up until he became a Paratrooper and was killed in action whilst still in his teens.

All I could do was repeat how sorry I was and to somehow try and comfort her by saying how proud she must be of him, but the tears and sobs continued.

She showed us photographs of his bedroom with his bed and football posters still on the wall, exactly the same as it was when he kissed her goodbye and left for the last time. His room was literally a shrine now, this poor lady will never get over the loss of her son and looking at his tender years I could understand why and I thought to myself, at least I spared my own Mother having to go through the same grief. Eventually she moved on to the seats in front of us and once again the reality of what we were doing and what we had been involved in, hit home.

Myself and Edward sat there in silence and contemplation, like back in 1982 on D Day when I climbed on-board the Sea King helicopter to go ashore, there was no going back now.

We banked to port, there was a strange silence in the aircraft as everyone was for a moment lost in their own personal memories, I heard the clunk of the landing gear lowering, my mouth felt dry and my heart raced, I felt a knot in my stomach, it was like I was looking into a black hole that was sucking me inside as I peered out of the window..

As we started our approach the Captain came on the tannoy and gave us all a surprise, it was not the usual altitude, temperature and time of arrival; it was when he announced, *The last time I was flying over here we were dropping bombs on the airfield at Stanley.* We were being flown by Bob Tuxford RAF Falklands War Victor tanker pilot, who flew the last leg from Rio Brazil to MPA. I personally felt it was a great honour and a privilege to be on the same aircraft as this man, and knew we were in safe hands, plus seeing the RAF Tornadoes escorting us in made me feel better, once I realized they were RAF and not Argentinian.

Banking to port I looked out of my window and caught the first glimpse of the Falklands for twenty five years, it was a strange surreal feeling, hard to describe, it certainly was not the same reaction to when I was about to land for an all-inclusive holiday in Tenerife, it was as if I had gone through a time portal, I was anxious, probably even more so when as a young soldier twenty five years ago, I went ashore, well I was a naive nineteen year old then and had no idea what War was, only that it was an adventure that I was happy to be part of.

We landed at MPA (Mount Pleasant Airport) which was opened by Prince Andrew on, May 12th 1985, three years after the War. As the door opened and I exited the plane, squinting into the bright blue Falklands day, the first thing I noticed was the intense cold on my bald head and this was summer as opposed to the winter months that covered the duration of the fighting, you certainly do feel the cold more when you get older, well I do anyway.

Even though we were once liberators, we went through the immigration procedure, which is perfectly understandable, crossing the T's and dotting the I's before heading off to our respective destinations, mine and Edwards being *Hill Top Camp* in Stanley.

On the bus going out of MPA we passed the static display of a McDonnell Douglas F-4 Phantom jet XV409, one of the Paras chirped up with 'Is that a Phantom?' Edward, with his dry Scouse humour said, 'No mate it's a real aircraft,' which had everyone in stitches, apart from the Para, who didn't see the funny side of it.

The sky turned black in an instant like someone flicking a switch and we were bombarded by a hail storm, which made it a bit more like how we remembered things here.

After an hour or so we arrived at *Hilltop Camp,* and waited to see what our accommodation was like. One of the Scots Guards lads, had lots of bunches of keys to the porta cabins, some were multi occupancy, some were two man, once again quick as a flash, as soon as the guardsman held out a bunch for a two man cabin Edward practically snatched them from his hands, with a 'We will take that one,' The guardsman just laughed and said 'OK Pal, Nay worries,' so that white box was to be our home for the next week, which suited us fine as it was more private and we wouldn't be getting disturbed by drunks in the night like back in the block in Germany, it was warm had a shower and a toilet, plus we just had to line up at the cook-house for our food with the other servicemen, we had both lived in far worse places around the world that's for sure.

During my military service I had never been the sort of soldier that just blindly follows orders and had my own private taste's i.e. Punk Rock, that did not sit well with my senior officers and this trip would be no different, I'm not using PTSD as an excuse , but I needed my own space and to do things at my own pace, the rest of the Pilgrimage veterans would be more Regimented, which can be expected, as that's how the military likes things run, on time and most ex services would be quite happy in that environment again, but not Edward and I, we hired a 4x4 , we had money in our pocket's and even before we left the UK we knew what we both wanted to do on the islands.

Without using detailed map references, Edward had a very good idea of where his Rapier 31 Delta was situated at San Carlos; it was close to the shore line and not far from a farm settlement, so our first mission was to find the location.

Driving towards San Carlos once Edward saw the farm, he was confident where his position was, we parked up the 4x4 and walked up the gentle slope. Edward carefully scanned the area for signs. After around ten minutes he stopped and pointed, 'It's over there Mack, I'm sure of it,' moving a little further on Edward stopped again, looking at the ground, then out to sea then back towards the farm orienteering himself, we both stood there, even looking up at the skies, as if waiting for an air attack. 'This is it Mack, this was our position mate,' we both began to sweep the area, like some police officers at a crime scene looking for forensic evidence, then I saw what looked like a stone, I picked it up and brushed the mud off, 'Here you go mate, you might want this', I smiled and handed Edward a small round green metal firing cap, which was used to initiate the firing of a Rapier missile. 'Oh my God, I can't believe that was just lying there in the mud all this time', said Edward as he looked at in in disbelief like we had just found a gold sovereign.

We both immediately then dropped to our knees to look for more treasure, like some crazed metal detecting freaks, only we just had our bare hands not a metal detector, first we saw the tip of an iron bar, so we pulled that out and used it as a makeshift shovel, digging into the soggy peat, it certainly brought me back to the day we landed as young soldiers, frantically digging our trenches, for protection from the air attacks. Then Edward noticed a piece of cam netting poking through the mud, 'Fuck me mate, look it's our cam nets', as he pulled at the netting like a fisherman pulling in his catch.

There were also a few tins of compo rations, which we probably could have eaten if we wanted , I'm sure Bear Grylls would have been pleased with our find, well maybe not, but he does like to eat some weird shit.

The next thing that happened was totally surreal, it was as if we were making a movie and this was a scene and the director shouted Action, out of nowhere an RAF Tornado jet screamed directly above our heads doing a roll as if to salute us or maybe he was just fucking frightening us. I stumbled backwards unsteadily in shock, even though part of my brain realized it was one of ours, part of my brain didn't, falling onto barb wire from the trench I cut my hand , ironically that was the first time I had spilt my own blood on the Falkland Islands.

On our way back to our vehicle, we decided to pay a visit to the farm, in the settlement, Edward, knew the couple from 1982 when he became and unlikely neighbour, we knocked at the door and were greeted like long lost sons, we stuffed our self with cakes and cups of tea and reminisced about the War and put the world to rights, meeting the Islanders and them showing how much they respected what we did for them, was heart-warming and just reinforces our belief that the liberation was justified, not that I ever thought anything different. Eventually with full bellies we waved them farewell and went back home to our white box at Hill Top Camp.

As for visiting my Rapier position, it was further up on in the mountains and I sadly didn't have the exact coordinates, with all the trials and tribulations around coming back I did not investigate contacting the Regiment , so I wouldn't be going to my position at San Carlos, but I would be going to the fateful position at Fitzroy.

This position would be much easier to locate, unlike the rest of the Pilgrimage organised trips, we just jumped in the 4X4 and set off, it was an amazing journey along the winding, bleak sixty eight miles, we could stop when we wanted and take our time, that's how we wanted it, I brought with me a bottle of red wine, this was to symbolically pour on the ground at Fitzroy , and a cross and a letter I would leave there , telling people about Mickey Quinn and how he was there with me that day.Like many of us, certainly psychologically, but as this was no ordinary road trip and a one off I would never experience again.

As I sped along the loose shale road, I took a swig of wine, almost loosing traction with the road, looking out of the window we had been joined by a group of galloping wild horses, another magic moment, we could have been on another planet at that time, whooping and screaming and laughing, we bounced along with the beautiful horses, I had already cut my hand, so a car wreck was out of the question, that would have been an ironic way to die especially here, well for us anyway. It was only one swig of wine, more symbolic really, I certainly don't drink and drive back in the UK, but this was very different, this was a Requiem for a soldier, or maybe more of an exorcism?

After what seemed like a million sheep later we saw the signs for Fitzroy, our horse friends had parted company and I slowed down, so I didn't take the wrong turning, one good thing was, if you did go wrong it was easy to do a U-turn on these desolate roads, and not a speed camera in sight. Then all of a sudden through the hail storms and mist, the sun came out like a biblical sign from the heavens and I was once again back at the one place in the world that had become a constant thought in my head and nightmares for the last twenty five years.

Parking up we noticed there were several other veterans and some family members who had lost loved ones gathering around the monument near the shore line, not wanted to intrude we kept a reasonable respectful distance, as we didn't know what private ceremonies were being carried out, then we saw our old troop commander, Lt Waddle, who went on to become a Colonel, eagerly we approached him to catch up. A smile lit up his face when he saw us and we all shook hands.

'Hello Sir.'

'No need for the Sir anymore, Adrian will suffice.' he laughed. But I found it hard to call him by his Christian name, even though we were all civilians now, I tried but 'Sir' kept coming out of my mouth, just force of habit and of course my respect for the man. He had gone on to earn his red beret and Para wings, but I noticed he still wore his 'Crap Hat,' dark blue beret that he wore when he was our boss, which I thought was a lovely touch and showed also the respect he had for his lads. I asked him if he had any photographs of us?

'Any photographs I have of the troop did not include you two, you were always skiving off and up to no good as usual.' We all laughed this, but he was right.

A younger lad was also stood at the monument, with a sombre face, in deep thought, we learnt later that he was the son of one of the Welsh Guardsman killed; I truly hope going to the Falklands has given him some closure.

Another man approached us and introduced himself, he was also a Guardsman and we chatted about the day's events, I explained who I was and he was extremely sympathetic, I was slightly taken aback, when he hugged me and said 'It's not your fault Tony, nobody blames you.'

This gentle display of emotion, was the nearest I came to shedding tears that day, but for some reason I kept my composure. I was surprised when I found out later that he had lost both of his legs, I could not tell at the time, as he had got so used to walking on prosthetic limbs.

Walking over to the monument on my own, I said a private prayer for those lost and also for Mickey Quinn, kneeling down I placed small wooden cross in the ground with a letter sealed in plastic, telling everyone about how and why Mickey died due to his PTSD and the Falklands War, then I took the wine and poured some onto the ground, 'Cheers Mickey,' I then took a drink myself. *'Pour La Mort,'*

Adrian and Edward had been watched me and when I walked back over, they asked if I was OK, then Adrian, said 'Anthony, would you like to walk with me?'

he gestured for me to follow him, as he set of up the hill in the direction of where we thought our Rapier had been.

As we walked on our own, he asked me, how I was, and what's it like to be an author and how many millions I had made, I laughed and reassured him that Id not made enough for a wet weekend in Blackpool.

Once at the top of the hill, he looked around and asked if this was were 32 Alpha was situated. I orientate myself by looking out to sea, at the lay of the hills in comparison to the settlement buildings, and tried to imagine myself sat on the tracker seat twenty five years ago and the view from my optics.

'Yes Sir I think this is about right.'

Both sitting down on the damp earth, he let out a long sigh of breath, shaking his head.

'What the hell happened Anthony?'

'I was tracking the lead Skyhawk Sir, I had him, but then we got systems fault.'

'So sad, so sad, but we did what we could, we should be proud of what we achieved and at the very least we won the War, things could have been a lot worse.'

Then Adrian stood up and brushed the grass of his trousers. 'Come on let's go and get a brew, or something stronger.'

It felt as we both walked back down to the people milling around below that we had just been to a funeral, which is in a lot of ways it was just that.

'Your right Sir, I mean Adrian, and don't call me Anthony, Mack will do,' I said laughing trying to lighten the mood. The Gunner and the officer twenty five years later, just two men, sat on a hill sharing a bond and memories that will never be broken or forgotten.

The last thing I did when alone, was take out a small green plastic American GI toy soldier from my pocket, one of those I played with as a young boy in my garden and buried it, I was symbolically burying part of myself.

Adrian, Edward and I were to march again once again on November 11th in the capital Stanley and as if to permanently remind us of that Mother Nature ruled, the weather was very atrocious, sleet and hail. I was wearing my blazer, with a thin white shirt and was soon soaked to the skin and shivering, but I put on my best drill. We both laid a wreath that my local Royal British Legion had kindly donated.

Once again I felt immense pride as the Islanders clapped and cheered us, at being a soldier, especially one that had liberated this tiny part of Britain at the bottom of the world.

One strange thing did occur in Stanley; I decided to pay a visit to the local Catholic Church, I prayed (Excuse the pun) that the church would be empty and for my sins it was, not even a priest was around. Kneeling down I said a few prayers, then got up and left, on the way out I stopped, took my camera from my pocket and took a photograph of the Altar, just like all the other photographs I had taken.

When later that that day I opened up the camera, the photo of the Altar was still there, thinking nothing of it, I closed it again, but when I opened it the same photo was still there. Even after I took a photograph of something different, the only thing I could see on the camera was the Altar photograph. I suppose it all depends upon your beliefs, a sign from God or a fault with the camera? For me I'm going with the fault.

I'm not sure if Edward would have been better off going back down there on a more structured trip with *SAMA (82)*, and maybe staying with a family. Perhaps he stayed in the porta cabin at Hill Top Camp more for my benefit than his own. Some of the other lads did not seem as mentally scarred as myself and he may have had a more enjoyable time, if enjoyable is the right word?

There was a change in me for the worse after we bumped into some psychiatrists one day walking through Stanley, they obviously had an interest in mental health issues and Edward was telling them about his experience back at his Rapier position the other day at San Carlos. I was just stood listening; I cannot recall the exact conversation, but when Edward said something along the lines off, *I used to think PTSD was a load of bollocks until that RAF Tornado buzzed us,* I walked away in disgust got back in the 4X4 and slammed the door.

Things were different between us after that, we hardly spoke and I felt extremely depressed, I felt like even my best friend didn't believe PTSD was real, I just wanted to go home.

The week soon passed and the morning came for us to fly back to the UK. Edward had to check in an hour or so before me, I heard him get up, we had separate rooms, I lay in bed thinking he is bound to open my door and tell me he was going and that he would meet me at the airport, but he just left without saying a word.

On reflection I could have made the effort and made sure I spoke to him before he left, but I didn't.

It didn't help matters that we were not sat together on the flight home; as we would have had ample time to talk about our experience.

I hope that it did help people going back; one veteran it plainly didn't help was a Welsh Guardsman that had a nervous breakdown in the departure lounge, a terrible thing to witness for everyone as he was taken away to hospital, I often wonder how things worked out for him. He would have had to wait at least another week for a flight back to the UK.

Myself and Edward sadly did not have any contact for a further eight years ironically, when I went through some of the blackest times and needed a friend that understood me, like the time he was there for me on the

Norland when I was thinking of throwing myself overboard. I believe we both suffered unnecessarily during this period. I am happy to say that we are both now back in contact with each other and speak on the phone almost every day.

Whilst writing this book I received the news that Edward has been diagnosed with cancer and like a true warrior he is doing what soldiers do best and fighting on.

I know of some Falkland veteran's that make frequent trips back to the Falklands, if this works for them I am delighted for them. Personally I can't see myself ever going back. We all have our own ways of coping and we are all different and all experienced different things. Some veterans received the same medal as I did, but did not take part in the fighting, it's just how things went and I'm sure if called upon they would have fought bravely and with honour, but it is much more easier for them to go back to the Islands as they will not have the same memories and emotions. It would be similar to me going to visit the WW 2 beaches of Normandy, I would be there to show my respect to those that lost their lives for their Country, but how could I feel the same as a veteran that fought and watched his mates being killed on the beaches that day?

IT'S ALL IN MY HEAD

On the 26th November 2010 I married Linda, at a very modest ceremony; there were only seven of us in the room, obviously the happy couple, two witnesses, Linda's friend and of course the registrars. We had both been married before and had the big events with lots of people that don't really know you that well, but enjoy the booze and the food, we have all been there, this time it was just about us.

After a quick wedding meal at a local pub, we drove down to Manchester airport and on to our honeymoon cruise in the Caribbean, which was a dam sight more comfortable than the last time I had spent at sea, and a lot warmer. Like many sufferers I had learnt to manage my PTSD and to the casual observer they would not think that anything was wrong.

We had a wonderful two weeks, the ship was so stable, you sometimes forgot you were even at sea, as I told Linda about the Bay of Biscay and our epidemic of sea sickness. We had a balcony and I loved, sipping a cup of coffee and watching the gentle waves, which obviously did bring me back to my time on-board the *Geraint,* especially when we were in the calmer waters near Ascension Island. Happily there would be no Captains rounds on this cruise, but I could go for a run if I wanted to and I did use the gym a few times.

I couldn't help but notice that during the day when I was sunbathing, I got some funny looks, I imagined they were thinking, *Look at that shaven headed tattooed thug, I bet he is a drug dealer or something.* Maybe I'm paranoid as well as all my other problems, but it was different at night, when I was dressed in my tuxedo and dickey bow and miniature medals, the vibe seemed very different and the other guests we much more welcoming and eager to chat. It's the old judging a book by its cover thing that we are all guilty of at some time or another.

Far too quickly we were both back home in Cumbria, with the obvious suntan and in my case probably and extra stone in weight.

On the 6th March 2012 we decided to make our family larger and bought a yellow puppy Labrador, I fittingly called him Gunner. On the 30th March 2012 I was in hospital after I attempted to commit suicide by throwing myself out of the bedroom window. It had nothing to do with the dog.

One morning I literally woke up with an incredibly loud ringing noise in my head that would not stop, it was as if I was still asleep in some terrible nightmare, PTSD is one thing but now this. How the hell could I stop the noise?

There is absolutely no doubt that if I had possessed a firearm I would have blown my brains out, but living in England as opposed to the United Sates, I didn't, so I opened the bedroom window and threw myself out, hoping it would kill me and the noise would stop.

As you will have gathered I didn't kill myself and only managed to break my leg and suffer sever bruising, with hindsight, I suppose I should have dived out head first.

For almost the next year of my life which included my fiftieth birthday I was hospitalised and I have no doubt that the stress I caused my wife, lead to her having a heart attack. From being happily married on a cruise of the Caribbean to this, why?

'TINNITUS.'

I always had a very faint ringing and hissing in my ears, due to firing rifles and artillery guns without the correct ear protection, but this was on another scale altogether.

I can only recall small parts of my time in hospitals; I spent long periods in a catatonic state. Catatonia is a state of neurogenic motor immobility and behavioural abnormality manifested by stupor It was first described in 1874 by Karl Ludwig Kahlbaum, in *Die Katatonie oder das Spannungsirresein* (*Catatonia or Tension Insanity*).

It goes without saying tinnitus and PTSD can be a deadly combination, especially for someone with an already fragile mind and mental health problems, just tinnitus alone can lead to suicide. Even as I type this it is raging, the only time I don't hear it is when I'm asleep, which also has its problems with night terrors, I'm always on the verge of panic and worry about suicide, I want to live, I have a reason to live, my wife, children, and for those that were killed in 1982. Without being over dramatic it's really is a miracle I'm still here.

The doctors could not seem to bring me back to reality, my wife told me that some of my friends came to see visit and I didn't recognise them. I was probably quite nasty towards them, I even said to my wife, you would be better of finding someone else and tried to give her back my wedding ring.

Running out of ideas the doctors asked Linda if she would be willing to try (ECT) treatment. This is where an electrical current would be sent thorough my brain under general aesthetic to purposely trigger an epileptic scizure. It was a last resort and it did seem to improve my mental state.

I recall very little about the events and when wife tells me things that happened to me it's like she is talking about a stranger, which at that time as an apt description.

Apparently I was at one time in every hospital in the County.

One of the side effects is memory loss and I have found this to be the case, I worry that I may have Alzheimers disease sometimes, like my late Mother. I can remember things from over forty years ago but seem to forget people's names and short term events, but I try to keep my mind as active as possible through my writing and poetry and I have recently published a book of poetry titled *Screaming In Silence,* which you won't be surprised to learn is trauma orientated. I hope that it may encourage other trauma sufferers to give poetry a try as it is useful as a tool of self-help and counselling. Sometimes we must go through great hardships and suffering to find inspiration and a way of telling our story and poetry seems a perfect fit for a serviceman or woman. All-though at one time I would have laughed at the suggestion as a young soldier.

PHOTOGRAPHS

EDWARD (L) TONY (R) STANLEY 2007

SAN CARLOS WAR CEMETERY

BOXING JUNIORS 1978 (L)

EDWARD , TONY, FITZROY 2007

NORTHERN IRELAND

HOME FROM WAR RAF WADDINGTON

FOOT PATROL NORTHERN IRELAND

32 ALPHA FALKLANDS WAR

32 ALPHA THREE KILLS

McNALLY FAMILY

END-EX

I want to reiterate that I had no problem going to war. It's what soldiers do from time to time, and we all knew that when we signed up. I have no problem, either, with soldiers dying or being injured in war – again, that's always a possibility. Of course, when the soldiers die or are injured because of a failure to ensure they have the best equipment available, which is a different matter. If our Rapier had been in good working order, maybe I would have been able to destroy one or more of the Skyhawk's that attacked the *Galahad*. If I'd managed to bring one of them down, maybe that would have put the others off. Maybe I would have missed altogether. We'll never know and in all Wars there are successes and failures. This book is obviously a based around the tragic events of the *Sir Galahad*, but we should not forget that my Rapier missile system also shot down three enemy aircraft, which I have no doubt saved British lives.

When soldiers are injured – whether visibly or mentally – as a result of warfare, the Army has a duty to provide the best care possible to help them recover.

Clearly, where lads have been shot or blown up, that means casevac-ing them to hospital immediately. The Army's record here is good – though the wider closure of military hospitals by the government is not good.

Where the injuries are less obvious, it means providing support and assistance to enable the soldiers to get better. The Army's record here is poor.

Over 250 young Britons died in the Falklands. Tragically, considerably more than that have since committed suicide. The South Atlantic Medal Association (SAMA82) said in 2002 that 264 veterans had taken their own lives. The toll can only have grown since then, though no-one seems to know the exact figure. When I came out of hospital I was visited by a Veterans Agency welfare officer, he said that he had involvement with several cases of Falklands veterans who's mental health had deteriorated after going back to the Islands.

Denzil Connick, the co-founder of SAMA82, believes PTSD is to blame.

Some people sneer at those with PTSD. Try sneering at Denzil: he was a Para who also lost a leg in the conflict, which shows the toughest of men can fall victim. Even SAS men have been among them – Charles 'Nish' Bruce was an SAS veteran and free-fall Parachute expert who committed suicide by jumping from a plane without a parachute. Frank Collins was another former trooper who killed himself. They and many others were said to be suffering from PTSD. Veterans comprise a disproportionate percentage of the homeless and convicted prisoners; many PTSD sufferers have gone on to commit serious crimes, so this is an issue which can affect even those with no link to the forces.

I'm not convinced the Army and the government have learned the lessons from the Falklands War. We've all heard tales of men dying in Iraq and Afghanistan because they had no body armour or because they were being sent into known landmine threat areas in thin-skinned Land Rovers, it took a lot of needless deaths before better armoured vehicles were provided– a scandal far worse than anything that ever happened to me. We know about the closure of the military hospitals, about the appalling state of MoD housing and the general cost-cutting and overstretch our forces face.

To my mind, there is no nobler thing that any many can do than to enlist to fight for his country and its causes; can the politicians who send our boys to war look themselves in the mirror and say they are doing their best by them?

I'd like the families of the soldiers who died aboard the *Sir Galahad*, and the survivors, to know that not a day has gone by since then when I haven't thought about what happened. I'm deeply sorry I couldn't do more for your sons, husbands, fathers and mates and I hope you can forgive me. We did our best and that's all anyone can ask.

Am I glad I was a soldier? As a small boy I played with my toy soldiers in the garden and even brought one to the Falklands and buried him with the real soldiers in 2007. That little boy fulfilled his dream and we all must have our dreams and ambitions. If I went back in time machine to the 60s, I would still pick up my toys soldiers and mud balls.

** ** *

War took another friend of mine in 2006, this time in Iraq. I met Dennis Brady during my time at British Cellophane and he joined after listening to me talking about Army life. Like me, he left and then re-enlisted, as a medic. Den died in a mortar attack on a British base in Basra Iraq in October. He, too, is sorely missed. R.I.P.

GLOSSARY

ACC – Army Catering Corps

AK47 – Russian Assault Rifle

ASM – Air to Surface Missile

BAOR – British Army of the Rhine

BC – Battery Commander

BOXHEAD – Slang for German

BQMS – Battery Quartermasters Stores

BSM – Battery Sergeant Major

CIV POP – Civil Population

DIXIE – Cooking Pot

DMS – Directly Moulded Soles

DPM – Disruptive Pattern Material

GPMG – General Purpose Machine Gun

GRUNT – Slang for Infantryman

LMG – Light Machine Gun

LSL – Landing Ship Logistic

MPA - Mount Pleasant Airport

MT – Motor Transport

NBC – Nuclear, Biological, Chemical

NISR – Northern Island Search Report

NITAT – Northern Ireland Training Advisory Team

NORAID – Irish American Fund Raising Organisation

PIRA – Provisional Irish Republican Army

QRF – Quick Reaction Force

RAMC – Royal Army Medical Corps

RE – Royal Engineers

REME – Royal Electrical Mechanical Engineers

RFA – Royal Fleet Auxiliary

RMP – Royal Military Police

RPG7 – Rocket Propelled Grenade

RUC – Royal Ulster Constabulary

SAM – Surface to Air Missile

SAPPER – Royal Engineers Soldier

SBS – Special Boat Service

SIGNET – Signals Network

SINN FEIN – Political Wing of the IRA

SLR – Self-Loading Rifle

SMIG – Sergeant Major Instructor of Gunnery

SOP'S – Standard Operating Procedures

SMG – Sub Machine Gun

SSAFA – Soldiers, Sailors and Airmen's Families Association

TA – Territorial Army (Now Army Reserve)

TC – Troop Commander

T'S & A'S – Tests and Adjustments

TSM - Troop Sergeant Major

VCP - Vehicle Check Point

WRAC - Women's Royal Army Corps.

Printed in Great Britain
by Amazon

82835256R00220